PRIVATE
12768

MEMOIR OF A TOMMY

PRIVATE
12768

MEMOIR OF A TOMMY

JOHN JACKSON

TEMPUS

First published 2004

Tempus Publishing Limited
The Mill, Brimscombe Port,
Stroud, Gloucestershire, GL5 2QG
www.tempus-publishing.com

British Library Cataloguing in Publication Data.
A catalogue record for this book is available from the British Library.

ISBN 0 7524 3184 6

Typesetting and origination by Tempus Publishing Limited
Printed and bound in Great Britain

CONTENTS

FOREWORD

There is not a shortage of personal accounts from the First World War. Most of those who fought may not have been poets, but they could read and write. The war stood on a cusp. Compulsory primary education ensured basic levels of literacy. A couple of generations later and the primacy of the written word would be challenged by other forms of communication. True, there are fewer narratives by private soldiers than by officers. But that still does not make John Jackson's story unique. So why publish another memoir?

The principal reason is the tone of enthusiasm, pride and excitement conveyed by its author. Conditioned by Wilfred Owen's poetry and dulled by the notions of waste and futility, British readers have become used to the idea that this was a war without purpose, fought by 'lions led by donkeys'. John Jackson was a lion. He served on the Western Front from 1915 until the war's end. He was present at Loos in 1915, on the Somme in 1916 and in Flanders in 1917; he was on the receiving end of the German offensive in Flanders in April 1918, and he took part in the breaking of the Hindenburg Line at the end of September 1918. For much of that time he was a regimental signaller, crawling over open ground ensuring that telephone links were maintained despite falling shells and small-arms fire. He was awarded the Military Medal for his bravery on the Passchendaele Ridge, the furthest point of the British advance in the third battle of Ypres. Those who doubt the value of decorations for gallantry, and their effects on morale, will suspend their cynicism when they read Jackson's reactions.

There are lions in this account, but there are no donkeys. Jackson's view of officers was conditioned by those whom he met, and they were largely front-line soldiers like himself. His account of the death of his commanding officer, Lieutenant-Colonel A.F. Douglas-Hamilton, who won a posthumous Victoria Cross at Loos for his brave leadership on 26 September 1915, shows his admiration for his superiors. Again and again throughout his narrative, he bears testimony, both direct and indirect, to the fellow-feeling and mutual respect that existed between officers and other ranks, and between the soldiers and their non-commissioned officers.

That was in large part the achievement of the regiment to which John Jackson belonged. In 1881 the regular infantry regiments of the British army were linked to form two-battalion regiments, with one battalion serving at home and one abroad. There was one exception to this rule, the 79th or Cameron Highlanders. This was good news for the Victorian lovers of kilts and bagpipes (and John Jackson proved to be just as much a fan as they), but it presented a major recruiting challenge as the northwest of Scotland could no longer produce sufficient men to fill so many Highland battalions. They therefore looked elsewhere in Scotland, to its industrialised central belt, poaching men that regiments from the Lowlands and borders reasonably regarded as their own. When the First World War broke out, Jackson was working in Glasgow with the Caledonia Railway. He himself hailed from Cumberland. But he joined the Camerons. His choice was determined, he tells us, by 'the class of men joining the various units'. Before the war, military service did not attract respectable men in secure and skilled employment like Jackson. During the war such people were anxious to serve alongside those with similar backgrounds. Jackson chose wisely. Initially destined for a Territorial Battalion, the 5th, he eventually found himself in the 6th. The University of Glasgow still awards a Cameron Highlanders prize each year. It was established as a memorial by those students from the university who joined the

8

6th Battalion in 1914 and came back from the war in memory of those who did not. It would be easy to conclude that relations in the 6th Battalion were good and morale high because of this mix of middle-class and skilled working-class backgrounds, and that may be right. But in 1916 Jackson was transferred to the 1st Battalion – the 'real' 79th and a regular unit. There is no indication that fellow-feeling was any different here.

Those interested in the operations of the British Expeditionary Force and its tactical development will find many significant insights in Jackson's experiences. His introduction to the front in 1915, at a time when the army was not under the strain it took later in the war, is striking for its good sense and its gradual nature. His criticisms of the behaviour of the men of the 21st Division at Loos, who he says were kept in the line at revolver-point by their officers, puts the fall of Sir John French, the commander of the British Expeditionary Force, in a different light. French was criticised for not having straightaway released his reserve, which included the 21st Division, to the General responsible for the battle itself, Douglas Haig. The division had a trying time getting to the front, but Jackson's narrative raises the question of whether it would have been of any use if it had got there earlier.

In 1916 Jackson was invalided back to 'Blighty'. His account of his recuperation and re-training is illuminating. He says that veterans, as he was now deemed to be, were treated with a light hand at home. When they got back to France they went through the infamous 'bull-ring' at Etaples. This was where, in 1917, the British army's only major mutiny of the war erupted. Jackson confirms that many of the non-commissioned officers 'took a delight in making things as hard as possible'. This angered those who had been in the front line before. But Jackson's account of the training itself leaves no doubt that it was purposeful and realistic: its toughness left its products better prepared for what awaited them.

Although Jackson took part in the advance to the Hindenburg Line (or Siegfried position as the Germans called it) in February 1917, in many ways his most interesting observations for that year concern the fighting that did not happen rather than what did. Haig's plan for the battle of Ypres involved an amphibious landing along the Belgian coast in the rear of the German positions. Jackson trained for an operation that would have broken the trench stalemate by using British seapower to get round it. But it was fore-stalled by the lack of progress further south, around Ypres itself, and by the subsequent deterioration of the weather as the season advanced. The 1st Battalion, Cameron Highlanders ended its share in the battle in the mud of a front line no longer marked by trench lines but by a string of shell holes.

In early 1918, it was still in the same sector, on the receiving end of German raids, launched to disguise where the true thrust of the imminent German offensive would be directed. On 21 March the Germans attacked further south, on the old Somme battlefield, but on 9 April a second blow fell in Flanders. It hit the sector of the line held by one of two Portuguese divisions. It crumbled, and the Camerons were one of the units put in to reinforce the salient to the south in a bitter defensive battle. Jackson later went on leave to Paris, whose cultural delights enchanted him (soldiers were tourists as well as fighters), and was then gassed. But he was back for the last operations of the war, the so-called 'hundred days' when the British army broke the Hindenburg Line and advanced north and east.

He leaves us in no doubt of his own sense of victory. The march towards Germany brought liberation to occupied France and Belgium. On 16 December 1918, with their colours brought out from storage in Edinburgh, the Camerons entered Germany with bayonets fixed and pipes playing. When John Jackson came to record all this, in 1926, he was sure that the cause had been right and that Britain had had to fight. He was writing before the flood of war literature triggered by Erich Maria Remarque's *All Quiet on the Western Front*. Between 1928 and 1930 novels and memoirs bore testimony to the sense of betrayal among those who had fought. Their difficulties in re-adjusting to civilian life, to a world without war, were linked to a revulsion against the war and the reasons for it. Many of them were victims of the Slump, unemployed and purposeless. Perhaps John Jackson himself went through similar disillusionments, but if he did he did not record them – or see fit to change what he had written in his memoir. By leaving it untouched he gave us a narrative which captures another perspective, written by somebody with no obvious agenda but possessed of deep traditional loyalties – to his country, his regiment and his pals.

Hew Strachan
Chichele Professor of The History of War at the University of Oxford
October 2003

A NOTE ON THE TEXT

This is a faithful reproduction of John Jackson's original handwritten memoir. Any infelicities of spelling, grammar or language in the original manuscript have been replicated in this edition.

The Editor

Preface

In the following pages, I shall endeavour to give some description of army life during The Great War, in conjunction with some personal adventures during that period. Compiled partly from the diary I kept while on active service and partly from my own vivid recollections, I hope it may be of some little interest to all who chance to read it. The book is dedicated to the gallant 79th Regiment of Foot, 'The Queen's Own Cameron Highlanders', in whose ranks I saw 4½ years of active service.

John Jackson MM
1st Battn Cameron Highrs

1
War!

My story begins in the memorable month of August 1914, in the city of Glasgow, where I was employed in the service of the Caledonian Railway Coy. Little need here be said of the events, which are now historical, leading up to the declaration of war against Germany, by Britain; chief of which were the Sarajevo assassination, followed later by the violation of Belgian neutrality by the hordes of the Hun, in their effort to capture the Channel ports, at a first lightning stroke. Let it ever be remembered, that but for active British intervention so early as August 4th 1914, this country of ours would not now hold her proud position as 'Mistress of the Seas', nor would there exist today the wonderful British Empire. Instead, German 'Kultur' would dominate us all, and only those who saw it in force, in the parts of France and Belgium occupied by German forces, can understand the humiliation such a situation would have entailed. The declaration of war caused tremendous excitement throughout the country, resulting in magnificent displays of patriotism on every hand. Perhaps for once in my life, I, too, was excited, as I knew it would mean a terrible fight. The spirit of adventure was always strong in me, and as news came of the departure of the British Expeditionary force, and the manner in which it met, and fought, 'a thin line of khaki', against the massive German columns, I knew the time had come when I could not live at peace as a civilian. A family bereavement stayed me some little time, but I was determined to go and fight, and stated my intention to enlist while on a visit home. I am proud to record there was no opposition to my wishes, though what the consequences might be, no one could foretell.

Two days later, on Sept 8th, along with a friend, Andy Johnstone, I went to the recruiting office in Cathcart Road, and there we signed on for '3 years or the duration'. We were sworn in and passed the doctor, and I remember the chief qualification necessary seemed to be our willingness to fight; certainly there was no real medical examination. At the recruiting office we joined company with two ticket-collectors from the Central Station, all four of us deciding to stick together as long as possible. Their names were Malcolm McLeod and Joe Symes.

2

I join the Cameron Highrs

In these early days of war, recruits had the choice of regiment they wished to join, a privilege which was denied to many thousands of men, who came under the law of compulsory service, as time went on. Had I enlisted in my own district, most likely I should have entered the Border Regt and probably this story would not have been written.

On the 10th Sept I reported, as instructed, at Maryhill Barracks, and, with my three companions discussed what regiment we should join, meanwhile taking notice of the class of men joining the various units, and finally decided on the Queen's Own Cameron Highlanders – the 79th Foot, a choice of regiment which I never regretted. The barrack-square was crowded with recruits, and a very simple method was put into operation for the purpose of placing men in the battalions they wished to join. At frequent intervals, long poles bearing a crude banner, on which were inscribed the names of regiments, were hoisted in the square, and men 'fell in' according to their choice. Here were to be found all the signs of cheeriness that have been the 'hall-mark' of the British soldier during the hardest campaign ever fought. Everybody was in high spirits, for this crowd was part of 'Kitchener's Army' in the raw; no need for compulsion here, and no conscientious objectors included in their ranks. The words of such a famous soldier as Lord Kitchener – 'Your King and Country need you' – were sufficient for the cosmopolitan crowd that we were. Workers of all grades, students, doctors, policemen, gentlemen-about-town, dukes' sons and cooks' sons all united under the motto, 'For King and Country', and all ready to see the game through to the end. Having had our papers examined, the men for the Cameron Hrs, to the number of 300, paraded at 8pm and left Maryhill by special train at 9.15pm. Our immediate destination was unknown, but we rightly judged it to be Inverness, that being the headquarters of our regiment. We created a stir at Perth, our first stop. As yet, there was no discipline amongst us, and being a lively lot, we made things hum. Apart from this the journey was uneventful, being night-time, and most of us tried to sleep. About 5am we reached Inverness, and marched to the castle over ground covered with snow. We had a miserable breakfast of bread and cheese and some half-cold tea. There was no sitting down to tables or being waited on. It was simply a wild scramble, such as respectable people could not imagine, and a very rough introduction to army life. It was no use waiting till the scramble had subsided. That only meant we should get nothing, so, like hundreds of others had to do, I scrambled for food. During the day we paraded, and each received a regimental number the figures 12768 being tacked on to my name. Afterwards, I had a walk through the town. Inverness is quiet, and clean.

From the castle, which stands out prominently on high ground, magnificent views of the in-lying country and the shores of the Moray Firth can be obtained. The barracks themselves are fine stone buildings, with spacious courtyard or square, for parade purposes. During the afternoon volunteers were called for to join the 5th (Lochiel's) Camerons, then lying at Aldershot, and as this seemed to us to be a step in the direction of France and the fighting line, we four gave in our names, and received orders to be ready to leave by the 4.20pm train, so that we were less than 12 hours at our depot. The volunteer party consisted of 100 men, and headed by the depot band, we marched down from the Castle to the station. Like many thousands of others, we had a rousing send-off from the people of Inverness, who showed the greatest enthusiasm, while the liveliness of our party was undoubted.

On a fine, September, evening, then, we set off on our journey south, and in the light of a summer sun we viewed the magnificent scenery, as the train ran through the Highlands. Towering mountains of rugged grandeur, their tops glistening with snow, peaceful glens and valleys, swift rushing streams that leapt and foamed among the rocks, and calm lochs in their moorland settings, left a picture in the memory which nothing could surpass. With a speed that made us hold on to the seats we swept through the Trossachs, and the famous pass of Killiecrankie, and as the twilight faded into darkness we arrived at Perth. During a stay of 20 minutes, we were lavishly supplied with hot tea, scones and cakes by ladies of the British Women's Temperance Association. For this kindness we were all very grateful to the ladies concerned, and gave them a rousing good cheer as our train steamed away from the platform on its way south. Reaching Carlisle in the early morning, we halted just long enough to change engines before continuing our journey via the L.N.W. railway to London. Here, after a cup of tea, which was all we had in the way of breakfast, we passed by way of the 'Tube' to Waterloo Station, and having some time to wait for our connection, many of us had our first walk on the streets of London. Soon we had entered on the last stage, and in due course reached the great military centre of Aldershot, after a journey occupying 21 hours. On arrival at the barracks, all the men belonging to the Western Highlands were asked to step forward. I believe there were two, and these were the only men out of the party sent specially to join the 5th Battalion who actually entered its ranks. The remainder were marched off to the gymnasium in Maida Barracks, which was to be our temporary residence. This was the beginning of the roughest period of my experience as a soldier at home. We were each given a boiled potato (skin included) and a piece of meat for our dinner. We did not have plates, knives, or forks, nor yet tables to sit at. No, our tables were the floor-boards. Perhaps allowances should be made at this time, for the unpreparedness of the authorities, with regard to the abnormal numbers of recruits, but with all things considered it was sickening to men, who had previously known decent home-life. We became more like animals than humans, and only by scrambling and fighting like dogs were we able to get food to eat. Some may read this and imagine that I exaggerate, but men who went to Aldershot in 1914 know I speak the truth. Our bedding was a solitary blanket, and our bed the block-paved floor of the gymnasium, so our training to withstand hardships began on arrival. Fatigued, as we were with our long journey from the north, we slept soundly, though perhaps many of us dreamt, that first night, of the good soft beds we had left at home.

3

Forming the 6th Battalion

At the time of my arrival at Maida Barracks, there were some 500 men, who did not belong to any particular battalion at all, and as the 5th Camerons had completed their strength, sanction was given to raise another battalion which came to be known as the 6th Camerons. A skeleton formation was made the day following our arrival, and we four friends, still determined to stick together, were placed in the third or 'C' company. When all the arrangements were completed, we were dismissed for the day, it being Sunday. It must not be forgotten that we were all wearing civilian clothes, many indeed wore their best, so we did not look much like soldiers of H.M. Army. In the evening we were given a kit-bag, and some minor articles of kit. For some time very few of us had such a thing as a towel; we learned to make a handkerchief do. We found Aldershot to be a hive of soldiers in different stages of training. In addition to the various regular barracks, camps had been formed wherever space could be found. As a training centre it is splendidly situated, and fashioned on modern ideas and requirements. Each barracks is complete in itself, from its officers' and 'married' quarters, to a well appointed cook-house and general offices.

Recreation grounds, then used for encampments were everywhere, also comfortable recreation rooms and reading rooms. A well known building in Aldershot was the 'Smith-Dorrien' Soldiers' Home, which contained a billiard-room, reading and writing rooms and a good library. In it were also a post-office, private baths, and a buffet, where light refreshments could be purchased. The 'Home' was always crowded when men were off duty, and many thousands of men will have pleasant recollections of happy evenings at the Smith Dorrien Home. The different barracks were separated by splendidly kept drives, which were bordered by gardens and shrubberies. At Farnborough, just outside the camp, airships and aeroplanes could be seen manoeuvring and flying about like huge birds. To us, from the north, all this was new and extremely interesting. The surrounding district, bordering on the 'Downs', was very much different from what we had been accustomed to, while the weather was fine and sunny. Immediately following the formation of the 6th Camerons, we commenced the drill, so necessary to make us efficient soldiers. We found it very hard, fatiguing work at the beginning, as we learned to march, form fours, about turn, and all the mystifying movements of that bane of recruits life, 'Squad Drill'. Our instructors were chiefly old reserve soldiers; indeed we were very fortunate in having so many who had served in the senior battalions of our own regiment. One of these instructors I remember especially well as he became my company Sgt Major at a later date. This N.C.O. appeared before us one morning, and it was very evident, despite the fact that he wore a nice grey suit, what his business was. He was very smart and very strict, but knew his work thoroughly and turned out some very smart squads. A few days later we were introduced to yet another ex-regular, dressed in blue serge, and carrying a silver mounted cane. This was John Macdonald late Regimental-Sergeant-Major of the 1st Battalion, a terror to recruits, and all under him on parade, but a gentleman off it. He became known to us as 'Jake', and when after a months stay, he left us, he was promoted to commissioned rank as Qr Master of the newly formed 8th Battn. As most days for some time were identical, a description of one will give a fair idea of the work we did at this period. Reveille went at 5.30am, and after a cup of coffee we turned out at 6.30 for what we called running parade. This consisted of a steady trot, or 'double', and short walk alternately, finishing up with a few minutes physical drill. We breakfasted at 8, and turned out again at 9.30 for squad drill till 12.15pm. Then dinner and parade at 2pm for more drill till 4.15pm. This ended our days work unless we were unlucky and got detailed for some 'fatigue' or work party. 'Last Post' sounded at 9.30 and 'Lights out' half an hour later, so we learned to keep respectable hours. Under our open-air life we became very bronzed and hardened. A great trouble, to many fellows, was sore feet, and the gravelled parade grounds of Aldershot were ideal places for raising blisters and making the feet uncomfortable. I was very lucky in having sound feet, and suffered little in this respect during all the campaign.

4

Rushmoor Camp

Having, through the addition of various drafts, become a larger body of men than the gymnasium was capable of accommodating, we left Maida Barracks on the 23rd of September for a camp at Rushmoor, on the outskirts of Aldershot. Life in tents under good conditions is fine, but it is not very nice when 14 or 15 men occupy one tent in hot weather, and it *was* hot at this time. What was much worse, we found the whole camp in a verminous condition, and we became very much infested with 'small mites of the crawling and biting variety'. We had no beds to sleep on; two blankets constituted our total in bedclothes, and our boots served the purpose of pillows. Near us were camped the 9th & 10th Gordons, the 11th Argyll and Sutherlands and the 13th Royal Scots. Soon after our arrival at Rushmoor, the rumour went round that the King was to pay us a visit, and we began practising formations for his inspection. We had our 'Royal Review' on Sept 26th on the 'Queen's Parade' Aldershot. 120,000 men were present, many of whom, like ourselves, wore civilian clothes. I remember that I wore the linen collar I had on when I joined up, but for this occasion I turned it wrong side out to appear as respectable as possible.

The day was very hot when the Royal visitors arrived. The Camerons had position on the left flank, and I was lucky enough to be in the front rank. First of all came the King attended by Lord Kitchener, easily recognised by his immense size. Following these came the Queen and Princess Mary with two Court Ladies in attendance. In rear of the Royalty were Sir A. Hunter, Chief of the Aldershot Command, and his Staff. The Royal party I had seen before, but I was very pleased to have the opportunity of seeing the great soldier, Lord Kitchener. Very stern and commanding he looked as he passed along the ranks, a centre of interest to the thousands standing to attention on parade. At the conclusion of the review, three mighty cheers were given for their Majesties, after which we marched back to the camp, the rest of the day being spent as a holiday. Shortly after this, we experienced a very welcome change in our drills. From the monotony of 'squad drill' we passed on to 'extended' or 'skirmishing order', as it was more popularly called, which allowed us much more freedom of movement. We learned to work to signals instead of commands, and began to get more interested in soldiering. Night operations were also introduced, while once or twice a week we went route-marching. This latter was perhaps the only parade one could say we really enjoyed, as it gave us opportunities of seeing round the surrounding district. We were encouraged in the practice of singing on the march officers and men joining in together. A great favourite was 'Auld Reekie', the only verse of which ran as follows:

> Oh! I can't forget 'Auld Reekie'
> Dear old Edinburgh 'Toon'
> For I left my heart behind me
> Wi' bonnie Jessie Broon
> But I'll wear a sprig o' heather
> When I'm on a foreign shore
> To remind me of 'Auld Reekie'
> And the lassie I adore.

To this and many other songs we marched many a mile along country roads of sunny Surrey, and Hampshire. As time went on the battalion. became possessed of a pipe band which evoked rounds of applause as it played through the villages.

Autumn was now advancing, with its shortening days and dark evenings, and the want of means of recreation was very much felt in the camp. During the last few weeks of our stay at Rushmoor, concerts were organised, by some of the junior officers, and these were held once a week. The number of voluntary artists who came forward, and contributed to these entertainments was surprising, and included singers, pianists, violinists, comedians and dancers. Many a pleasant evening was spent in a large marquee, which served as a 'Hall' for our concerts. About this time we were issued with our first uniforms and a funny looking lot we were when dressed up. I got hold of a regimental tunic of scarlet, complete with blue cuffs and white facings, together with blue trousers sporting a red stripe. Camp life soon spoiled their appearance, but they were all we had for a long time. We were supplied also with rifles, and began to look like real soldiers. We had much useful instruction given us on the care and handling of our weapons and found ourselves having extra work keeping them clean. There was now a general break-down in the weather, and we found camp life anything but sweet, amongst rain and mud. Generally when it was wet we had lectures in marquees on the methods of fighting at the front, also on trenches and various other interesting items. Sometimes, however, we were caught out in the rain; I particularly remember doing a route march one day, 11 miles out and 11 miles back to camp, while it poured down. We had no overcoats, and nothing to change into on our arrival home, so we just had to grin and bear it. I suppose this should be termed the 'hardening process'. Dodging rain drops which came through the tents, was a favourite pastime in bed on a wet night, while it was a common occurrence to find water in our boots in the morning. The camp got into a terrible mess, and so did we as we floundered about amongst the mud. With the weather conditions so bad, we were daily expecting to be moved to better quarters but it was not till 16th November that we packed up at Rushmoor Camp. We learned we were going to one of the many hutment camps, which at this time were being built for the accommodation of troops in many parts of the southern counties. From Aldershot, we proceeded via the London and South Western Railway to a little station named Liphook. Detraining here, we marched to Bramshott Camp, situated on the London–Portsmouth road, now so well known as the training camp of thousands of Canadian soldiers. The 45th (our) brigade, with the 46th, were the first occupants of this famous camp, and we found it in a semi-finished condition on our arrival. A small army of men was busy erecting huts, while a continuous stream of motor wagons passed to and fro, carrying building materials, both for huts and roadways.

5

Life at Bramshott

I cannot admit, either from first impressions, or from our experience of it, that we ever cared for Bramshott Camp. The huts and their environs were nothing less than a quagmire, so much so that at times it was impossible to 'form up' on the parade ground and we had to make use of the main road, very often, for this purpose. We did a great deal towards making roads and pathways through the camp, work that we did not relish very much I must say, as the weather was generally very cold and wet. For our training ground we were allowed the use of the Wolmer Park estate, parts of which were eminently suitable for open-warfare training as it contained large tracts of scrub and moorland. We continued to progress in our musketry, and began to practise in shooting, commencing on the minature ranges. Great attention was still paid to our marching. We had now regular route-marches, and began to be well acquainted with the district. The roads were splendid to walk on, and we discovered many beautiful woods and interesting villages. A prominent feature of the district is the large number of road-side hotels, suggesting that the beautiful scenery succeeds in attracting many visitors during the holiday season. Not many miles from the camp, and along the Portsmouth road, is a very wonderful natural depression of the ground, having the curious name of 'The Devil's Punch Bowl'. It is like a huge cup with very steep sides and a circumference of about two miles. Many a fine imitation battle have we fought through the Punch Bowl, with its dense undergrowth, its fine trees, its whins and thorns that made you move on whether you wished to or not. Our night manoeuvres must have often alarmed the people of the peaceful south-country villages; to be wakened in the middle of the night by a wild rush of feet along the village street, accompanied by 'wild Hie'lan' yells' could not be conducive to calm sleep and pleasant dreams. Generally speaking, however, the inhabitants took everything in good part, and the majority thought a lot of the 'Jocks', which the exigencies of the war had brought among them. To help pass away the long winter evenings, a large marquee had been erected near the camp, and this we used as a reading and writing room. There was also one in which cinema shows were frequently given. Concerts too were organised, at which many local ladies were voluntary artists It was not uncommon, either, for a large party of men to be invited to a supper and social evening, by ladies of the outlying villages, such was the good feeling existing between the people and ourselves.

Christmas was now drawing near, and we began to think of 'leave', and a few days at home. In due course we went on furlough, and I well remember how we paraded in the early hours of a wintry morning, and marched down to Liphook Station, en route for London and thence home. For my part I was glad of the few days, which I spent among friends at home, though the time passed all too soon. Going on leave is very nice but the return to camp in this instance was a 'knock-out'. After a miserable journey back to Bramshott, via London, on arrival we found that the windows of our huts had been opened during our absence and our blankets were soaking with the rain which had driven in. Tired, and weary as we were, after our long journey, we could only pass the remainder of the night trying to keep warm by walking about the hut. Soon after this there arrived, in a draft from Invergordon, a young fellow who belonged to Kendal, by name of Charlie Hutchinson, and between us there sprang up a lasting friendship. He was allotted to my section and took the place in my immediate circle of friends, of Joe Symes, who for some trivial fault had been transferred to the Royal Scots Fusiliers some time before.

We began the year 1915 by having a holiday on New Year's Day, and enjoying a grand dinner given to 'C' company, by our popular company commander Captain Crichton. Needless to say we did full justice to the good feast provided. We were now busily engaged in our musketry training and for the purpose of firing our courses, had to tramp to Longmoor Range every day. I think we all liked range-firing, and competition was keen amongst us as to who could make the highest score. On January 22nd the whole of the 15th Division comprising (in infantry):

44th Bde:	7th Camerons, 8th and 9th Gordons & 9th Watch
45th Bde:	6th Camerons, 11th Argylls, 7th R.S. Fusiliers, 12th H.L.I.
46th Bde:	7th & 8th Seaforths, 7th & 8th K.O.S.B. and 13th Royal Scots

were reviewed on Frensham Common by Lord Kitchener and M. Millerand, the French Minister for War. From our camp to Frensham was a distance of 9 miles, and this we marched in the fiercest of winter weather. We carried no great-coats, although snow fell all day, and for 3 hours we stood waiting, numb and cold, for our visitors. Many a poor beggar fainted under the trying ordeal, and was carried off on a stretcher. Through the stampeding of an officer's charger, we were treated to a fine exhibition of horsemanship on the part of our transport officer, an ex-Canadian rancher, who succeeded in rounding up the runaway in true cowboy fashion, after an exciting chase on the common, to the cheers of 20,000 onlookers. Our struggle back to Bramshott through a foot of snow comes back to my memory, as clearly as if it happened yesterday, with the brutal voice of our second-in-command, the Earl of Seafield, forever ordering us to 'keep to the left', on a road which was little removed from a cart-track. The 1st of February brought to an end our range-firing, and thereafter we returned to our drills, our route-marches and fatigues. We had also had a large amount of trench digging, and this to many fellows unused to handle a spade, was a heart-breaking job. Always,

however, we had our fun as we worked and the startled exclama-
tion of a man engaged in trench work by night, as he found a pick
sent neatly through the seat of his trousers, taught one to be careful
as to who was working behind him. I'm sure officers must have
been forced to smile at what they heard sometimes under cover of
the darkness of night. We were now so well advanced in our training, that a half holiday was allowed us on Saturdays, and numbers of
men made use of the weekends to visit London or Portsmouth.
Sunday mornings found every available man on Church Parade.
The majority, belonging to the Presbyterian Church, attended a
massed brigade service, generally held in the open air. A small
number belonged to the Church of England, myself being one of
these few, and we were allowed to attend service at the parish
church at Bramshott, where we were always welcomed, and treated
with every courtesy. We had now reached the middle of February,
and rumours were current that we would soon be moved again. On
the 18th an advance party of Black Watch and Gordons of the 44th
Brigade arrived in Bramshott to take over our billets, while a party
of our own men left for Basingstoke. Certain now that we were
leaving Bramshott, our hearts grew light, and we did not mind the
numerous hard fatigues such a movement of troops entails. It was
whispered we were going into 'private billets' which meant a sort
of heaven to us, after our rough experiences at Rushmoor and
Bramshott. We cleaned and scrubbed our huts and bed-boards; in
fact everything that would scrub, got its share. We paid final visits to
the surrounding villages wondering perhaps if we should ever meet
such good friends again. To the villagers it was to be a sore parting,
their 'Jocks' were leaving them at last. We were the recipients of
sincere good wishes on every hand, but while regretting the loss of
such warm-hearted friends, I think none of us were sorry to say
farewell to the muddy precincts of Bramshott Camp.

6

Billeted in Basingstoke

At mid-day on the 20th of February we marched out of Bramshott Camp to the strains of 'The 79th's Farewell' played by the pipers, and entrained at Liphook travelling from there, via Petersfield, Redhampton, Porchester and Winchester to Basingstoke. On our arrival, it was found there was insufficient accommodation in the town for the whole regiment, and accordingly my company were billeted protem in the small village of Worting situated about 2 miles north of Basinstoke. I considered myself very fortunate in being allotted to the house of a signalman named Bradbeer, whose wife, a Devonshire woman, showed me the greatest kindness and I shall ever have pleasant memories of my stay with these people. It was of course a decided change for us to have a good house to stay in, and real, comfortable, beds to sleep in, accustomed as we had been for some months to roughing it in camp. As at Bramshott the people round about were all good to us, and spared no effort to make us feel at home amongst them. Concerts, whist parties etc, were arranged for our pleasure, thus showing the generous hospitality of these friendly south country people. About the end of the month the battalion was issued with its proper uniform of kilts and khaki tunics, and so at last we were able to dress as befitted a proud Highland regiment. I well remember our first parade in kilts; how smart we all appeared, and how the C.O. Col Douglas-Hamilton surveyed with evident pleasure, the ranks of his men as he passed up and down on horseback.

Accommodation having now been found in Basingstoke, my company was transferred to their new billets in town on March 12th. Again I had a splendid billet with a Mr Purdue in George Street, and had for a room-mate my good friend Charlie Hutchinson. Here again, our landlady was very kind, and everything was made very pleasant for us. Charlie and I often went to church services with Mr Purdue, a jolly good fellow, who did all in his power to show us all there was to be seen and known in the district. As often as possible we visited our good friends in Worting, where we were always made welcome.

Our military training was now reaching advanced stages. Route marching, always the most enjoyable of parades made us familiar with a large part of Hampshire, the length of marches being gradually extended till we were hardened to perfection, and it would have been a remarkable regiment that could have endured the pace and fatigue alongside of us on the march. 'A Cameron never can yield' was an appropriate motto for us, there was no 'give in' attached to the 6th Camerons. Night operations, too, became much in vogue, including trench digging, sham fights and forced marches, and from these hard nights we used to return to our billets at all hours, and Charlie and I were always ready for the hot cocoa, left ready for us by our landlady, before tumbling into bed. Our training, if hard, was very interesting, and allowed us much freedom of movement; moreover it kept us very healthy, and from the open-air life we were in a hard and splendid condition. We were fast becoming finished soldiers, and knew our time in this country would be short, but everyone was anxious to be out among the real fighting. Perhaps we did not fully understand what it meant, but we were full of enthusiasm and confidence in our ability as a regiment to make a good name once we had the chance. We had a brigade inspection on Basingstoke Common on March 18th, by Gen. Pitcairn Campbell, O.C. Southern Command, which passed off very well.

The scene of much of our training was the beautiful surroundings of Hackwood Park, the home of Lord Curzon, and it was here that the Queen of Belgium and her children were then staying as 'refugees' from the war. Field games were very much indulged in at this time, football being the chief attraction. We had quite a good regimental team, and many were the friendly tussles we had with the rest of our brigade, and also the local teams of the town. There was great rivalry between the Cameron team and that of the Argylls, the merits and performances of the two teams being about equal, and there was sure to be a battle royal when they met in games.

On April 3rd we were issued with new leather equipment which puzzled us for some time, before we got it correctly put together. This was something more for us to keep clean, and, of course was responsible for not a little 'grousing'.

Bayonet fighting now became very much in evidence, during this period in our training, as did also trench digging by night. Skirmishing and sham battles we always enjoyed whether by day or night, and we tramped many miles during these operations. I remember one day having a mimic battle at Winklebury, said to be the scene of a battle in old English history. Our objective this day was Winklebury Hill held by the Argyll and Sutherland Highrs, and after various manoeuvres, extending over some hours, we were adjudged to have been successful in our attack, and to have captured the position held by our rivals.

Our pleasant stay at Basingstoke could not last for ever, and after about six weeks we began to make preparations for yet another move. The trenches were all filled in at Hackwood Park and this took a good deal of work, though not nearly so much as it took to dig them. Once more we had to say 'Goodbye' to good friends, whose kindness will always remain a pleasant memory. We handed in our extra kit and blankets on Sunday April 25th, and made ready for moving next morning; the beginning of a march I'll never forget.

7

Chisledon Camp

The whole battalion paraded at 9am in full marching order and I think never did a regiment look smarter. I imagine I can see it yet, lined up in George Street waiting the arrival of our C.O., while in the meantime we received the good wishes of our friends. At length we were ready, a moment's silence, then the voice of the Colonel, 'By your right, quick march!' followed instantly by a deafening crash of drums, and to the music of the skirling bag-pipes we were off. As a tribute to our popularity the inhabitants of Basingstoke lined the road for some distance out of the town to have a last look at the lads whom they might not see again. After 50 mins of marching we had 10 minutes halt this being a recognised and necessary rule on the march. The day was fine with the sun blazing down on us from a clear sky and the roads hot and dusty. Strewn as they were with small sharp flints and shingle, the roads were not conducive to easy walking, but we were fit for anything in those days.

Taking a westerly direction, we passed through some lovely country, brilliant with the green freshness of spring, a country that lay undisturbed and at peace, and we caused no small wonder with our swinging kilts and skirling band, among the rusticated people of the villages en route. At mid-day we halted for 40 minutes near Kingsclere, and turned into a grassy field, where we had our lunch (bully-beef and biscuits), with a drink of water to finish off. It was a welcome relief to get rid of our heavy equipment, and to lie down on the grass and rest for a few minutes. The hard going was beginning to be felt, and there were many with sore feet, but a wash among the cool waters of a stream, among the osier beds gave much benefit, and soon we were off again. About 4.30 in the afternoon we arrived at the old town of Newbury in Berkshire, famous for its racecourse. We had a wonderful reception on our entry into the town, no doubt a Highland regiment was an unusual sight in this inland town. We were billeted on the people for the night, and I for one, was ready to turn in and have a good sleep. Our distance for the day had been 20 miles. Next morning we paraded at 8 o'clock, and continued our journey from Newbury at 8.45am. We struck a good road to Hungerford 9 miles distant, and leaving there we passed into the county of Wiltshire, finding the road gradually getting worse while the hot sun seemed to burn us up. Men began to complain about their feet and it was evident that the battalion was in great distress, but still there was no falling out, indeed the gameness of everyone was something worth seeing. The pipers, with so much continuous playing, were almost exhausted, but still we struggled on. A halt was made for dinner near the village of Aldbourne, and then we set off, grimly determined to finish our march, let the hardships of the road be at their worst.

Drawing near to our destination we were met by the band of the Royal Scots who had come to play us into camp. That regiment, together with the Argylls, and Scots Fusiliers, had made the journey by train, and now they were gathered to see how we had 'stuck it' by road. The new band, marching at the head of the battalion, seemed to put new life into our jaded limbs, and with a great rally we topped the last hill, and from its height looked down at the camp at Draycott, with a thankfulness that, at long last we were in sight of our destination. The last lap down the chalky hillside was a rough and rocky track, and I'm rather afraid that we staggered more than we marched for the last mile. We were in fact almost 'played out' and were glad to lie down and rest on the floors of our huts. Our distance for the second day's march was 28 miles, or a total of 48 for the two days. I have calculated that our actual marching time for the journey was 11¼ hours. Carried out as it was in full marching order, under terrific heat, and upon shingly roads, it was an achievement to be proud of, and was about the toughest march I ever had.

We found our camp was only in course of construction, and its situation lay not far distant from the town of Swindon. It had every appearance of becoming a fine barracks. Each hut, built of sheets of asbestos had its bathroom attached, while the offices, store-rooms, cook-houses etc, were very modern affairs. Our sister brigades the 44th and 46th were also in Chisledon Camp, so that at this point all the infantry of the 15th Division were met at last, which could mean but one thing, and that was an early departure for the fighting line. We soon set about our final musketry course, and then were put through some brigade and divisional training. We enjoyed our field days, sometimes through by the old town of Marlborough and along the Devizes road, or round about the villages of Wroughton, Ogbourne, and Ogbourne St George. Also we practised night assaults on various imaginary enemies, such operations always being taken seriously by us. We were anxious to learn, eager for anything that would fit us for our expected battles across the Channel. Our training now seemed to be complete, so we had a few extra days on the range, this time doing all our shooting with fixed bayonets which made the rifles much clumsier to handle. I could generally make good work with a rifle, and at times came out top scorer in the section. Firing 15 rounds per minute, I scored 9 consecutive 'bulls', 4 'inners' and two 'magpies', or 52 points out of a possible 60 at 300 yards. At 600 yards I had 10 'bulls' from 10 rounds which made a 'possible'.

8

Sports and a Royal Review

On May 19th we began our preparations for brigade sports. In the eliminating contests for the battalion I represented 'C' Coy in the 100 yards, but was beaten for a place in the final by Sgt McAllister, a really fine runner. In the half mile I was second to a Scottish ex-Amateur Champion, both of us qualifying for the brigade final. The brigade sports were held in a field near camp on May 22nd, which was in the nature of a gala day for us. The Brig. General had promised a silver cup for the regiment with the highest number of points. This added to the interest of the competition, and we Camerons vowed to make a bold attempt to win the trophy. The first item was the final of the half-mile, each of the regiments having two representatives. I had been suffering from the effects of a strained leg, and was in fact very lame. My pals wanted me to draw out of the race, but I wasn't giving in and so I lined up with the rest. The result of that race surprised even myself. At the half-distance I went to the front with a burst that surprised the other runners, and remained there to win by a couple of yards. I dropped as I broke the tape, and had to be carried off suffering terribly from my damaged leg, but I was proud to have scored the first 3 points for the Camerons; and I'm afraid I was treated like a hero for my share. Sgt McAllister won the 100 yards and ¼ mile, in fine style, and the silver cup was eventually well won by the Camerons with a total of 47 points against the Fusiliers, second with 23 points. At the conclusion of the sports, the prizes were presented by the Brigadier's wife, and I had the honour of receiving the cup on behalf of the regiment. On May 28th, we set off on a field day, and after a good deal of skirmishing, we dug trenches on the Downs, in which we had to stay the night. Rations were served out and each man made his own dinner. This, of course, seemed great fun to us. We spent a cold, weary night in those trenches, and we were glad when morning came, and we marched back to camp. I took advantage at this time of a weekend pass, and journeyed to Basingstoke to see old friends, who were very pleased to have me back for a short visit. On the last day of May, we went out on a great divisional scheme. Arrived at Marlborough we stayed for one hour, and I remember watching a cricket match in the College grounds. From Marlborough, we marched to Savernake Forest, and here we skirmished, and had mimic battles. In the evening we 'dug in', and were kept working at our trenches all night. We felt very hungry, having had nothing to eat since leaving camp, except a piece of bread and bully beef. In the morning, we carried on with the operations, and in the course of our advance, passed through a magnificent avenue of stately beeches, extending through the middle of the forest for a distance of 4 miles. Our scheme ended at the village of Bedwyn, where the 'enemy' was surrounded and captured, and then we had to march back again to camp arriving there in the late afternoon feeling absolutely done up. Much of our spare time these days was spent in seeing the country and roaming the 'Downs'. There were also the usual town attractions at Swindon, a short distance away. Great excitement was caused by the news that the division was going to Salisbury Plain for a Royal Review, and there was much cleaning up and ceremonial drill in preparation for the event.

We left camp en route for 'the plain' at 11am on June 23rd and, marching by way of Marlborough and Ogbourne, we continued westward to the village of Pewsey, and there halted for the night. Bivouacks were erected in a field, our one blanket being stretched over short sticks, after the fashion of a tent, while the ground made a bed. This, however, was no great hardship to us, after our march of 14 miles, we were glad to crawl inside our bivouacks and rest. 'Last Post' was sounded at the early hour of 8.30pm, but our sleep was of short duration, the pipers of the Royal Scots rousing us at 2.30am. By 4 o'clock we had breakfasted, and were on the road again, marching, via Eversleigh, to the inspection ground on the plain, where we arrived at 8.45am. At 11 o'clock the Royal Visitors arrived, accompanied by Kitchener and the usual array of Staff Officers. After inspecting the parade, the division marched past the saluting base, regiment after regiment in line, with bayonets fixed, the King taking the salute while the massed bands of the division played the regimental marches. It was a stirring display, for the division was splendid, and was greatly complimented in orders on its appearance. One thing in connection with the review, I can always remember, after passing the King, we marched for an hour with fixed bayonets. Any soldier knows the fatigue such a march means, and we were tired enough with the 20 miles we had already travelled that day. In the evening we halted near Wilcot, and, after another night spent in a field, went leisurely home next day feeling well tired out. Reviews may be grand affairs, from an onlookers point of view, but the men have to suffer all the hard work attached to these military displays.

We all understood now that this was the 'last act' before we went abroad. Leave was granted (last leave) in more senses than one it proved for many of us; two companies were sent home, and I was one of the lucky ones to get away with the first batch. Leaving Chisledon on June 26th and travelling via Swindon I went to

Cheltenham, a very nice town in which I spent some time while waiting for my train. From there I went on to Derby and Leeds, arriving at Carlisle in the early hours next morning. Knowing I would be far travelled before, (if ever) I reached home again, I spent a few busy days visiting friends, and it was not long till the time came for me to rejoin the regiment. I think the excitement of being home did much to hide the seriousness of my visit. Who could say if I'd ever come back; yet this never worried me. I was ready and my duty was plain. The last 'Goodbyes' over, I had a good send off from Carlisle on July 1st, as I returned to camp at Chisledon. It was a long weary journey back, and I arrived there to find the second half of the battalion ready to go on furlough. Many of the men of these two companies were decidedly unlucky, for in many cases when they got home, they found orders recalling them to the battalion immediately.

9

Off to the 'Front'

It was at 3am on Sunday July 4th, that orders came to camp for the 15th Division to mobilise. No one could attempt to describe the excitement which prevailed that morning, when the long expected news became known. In a way it was welcomed. For weeks and months, we had looked forward to this, though perhaps we had not considered all that we might have to go through, once we crossed the Channel However, the fighting spirit was strong in us; we were ready, trained to the last degree of fitness, and like hounds on a leash we strained to be at the great game across the water. Each man was medically inspected, and we received our overseas kit. It was at this stage I was made a cycle despatch rider and attached to Battn Hqrs. There was a section of 9 of us, and it is wonderful to think that we all fought throughout the war without one killed, though the Armistice found us scattered to many parts, from Inverness to West Africa, and from Irish camps, to the French fighting line, and beyond that to prisoner of war camps in Germany. The officer in charge of this section was 2nd Lt Roy Cameron the Signal Officer, a fine young fellow whom we all respected greatly. I remember the day before we left, after we had all been photographed, he made a short speech in connection with the work we might be called upon to do as part of our duties as despatch riders at the front. In this he urged us to forget that there was such a word as 'cannot' in our vocabulary, and that it must be our first duty to get our despatches 'through'. Had he been lucky enough to live to see the war over, I think he would have been proud of his cyclist section. We had a great farewell supper at midnight of July 7th, and the Hqr section, which included the cycle section, who were going in advance of the remainder of the battalion, left Chiseldon at 1.30am; slipping silently away in the darkness, and marched into Swindon, there entraining for Southampton, which we reached after an uneventful journey at 9am on the 8th.

The great port showed many signs of activity and our attention was directed to the vast number of ambulance trains that stood in the railway sidings. We watched with interest the arrival, in dock, of the hospital ship, and the long stream of wounded that were disembarked, and carried, on stretchers, to the trains in waiting. This was our first contact with the realities of war. Our cycles and equipments were placed on board the troopship SS 'Courtfield', and we had dinner on board. All the Hqrs of battalions in the division were now gathered together, and formed the advance guard of the division. The Cameron Highldrs detachment was under the command of Major Scott-Kerr, an officer who had already seen service in France, and who was slightly lame as a result of wounds received in action. We sailed at 5.30pm, accompanied by an escort of 3 Torpedo Boat Destroyers. Our Channel passage was uneventful and silent, and now that we were really off there were wistful looks astern as the coastline sank on the horizon. For many of us it was 'Good bye

England'; some of us would live to return, others would go down fighting. That was the inevitable result and such were the thoughts passing through our minds as the troopship drew steadily near to the shores of France, yet withal our fighting spirit remained high as ever. The 'Courtfield' berthed in the harbour of Le Havre during the early hours of the next morning and disembarkation commenced at 6am. There was much hurry and bustling about on the rough cobbled streets of the old French town, and we were greatly interested in our foreign allies, with their quaint old-fashioned clothes, and their chattering language, which was quite unintelligible to many of us. We seemed to be welcomed, however, and there were cheers and shouts of 'Vive l'Anglais', and 'Vive l'Ecossais'. Our officer in command gave us all a good breakfast at his own expense, for which we were all very thankful. Later we marched to a rest camp, and where thousands had been before us, we slept in tents for the night, being glad of the rest and sleep.

10
Our journey to the trenches

Next day, we were entrained in the goods station in horse boxes, and began to feel the first discomfort of railway journeys on active service. The vehicles were lettered on one end '8 Chevaux' and on the opposite end '40 Hommes', meaning 8 horses or 40 men, and so, trucked in forties we set off on the first stage of our journey to the fighting line. Our first stop of importance was the old town of Rouen on the banks of the River Seine. Proceeding at a very slow speed, we reached Boulogne at 9am on the 10th of July, and here joined the main body of the regiment, which had crossed by the shorter Folkestone–Boulogne route. Leaving the train we now set off to complete our trek on foot, and that night we found ourselves in some curious, and not too clean billets, mine, I remember being a cow-shed. Having already realised we were in for a rough time, it seemed best to accept things as we found them. On looking round we saw that the village was called Bayonghen, and here we stayed a few days, passing the time doing light training, and listening to lectures. It was during our stay at this little old-fashioned village that we received our first gas-helmets, these consisting of a kind of veil, with a pad, chemically treated to counteract the poisonous fumes of gas, made to cover the mouth and nose.

Although so far behind the actual firing line, we could at times hear the dull boom of heavy guns away in the distance, and this served to keep up our excited curiosity as to what was happening in front. Our stay in Bayonghen was of brief duration, and we were soon on the road to the trenches again. Our billeting officer Lieut McMaster, with three cyclists, including myself, rode ahead of the battalion to take over billets at our next halting place, another small village called Wallon-Capelle. On our way we passed through the town of St Omer, well known as British G.H.Q. Billeting proved to be a weary sort of job. We did not succeed in getting just what we'd like to have for the regiment, any place with four walls was regarded as a billet; it didn't matter about a roof. It was a sudden change from the comfortable camp we had recently occupied over in England, and it was well that the weather for the present was fine. We found that the French roads, with their square paved blocks were not good for marching upon, and after a 15 mile tramp the battalion was ready for a sleep, no matter what the surroundings might be. Wallon-Capelle held us for one night only, and at 6am I was off again in attendance upon the billeting officer. About noon we arrived at Ham-en-Artois, a large village, but on enquiry we found there were no billets to be got. This seemed a sad state of affairs, but we were learning day by day what 'active service' meant. Later in the day the battalion arrived in the village and bivouacked in a field by the roadside. We had no covering except a waterproof sheet, and to make things worse it began to rain heavily. I had to take up the duties of orderly, between our own and Brigade Hqrs, and did not finish till midnight. Tired out, and wet through, I tried to find a decent place to lie down, but there was nothing for it but the wet field to sleep on. In the morning, I awoke to find myself surrounded by the waters of a flooded stream. That, however, had not prevented me from having a good sound sleep. On July 17th we again went forward, passing through the fairly large town of Lillers on our way. After a ten-mile tramp, we reached the village of Hesdigneuil, and here we again erected our 'bivvys' in a field. That night, I was sent off with despatches for the 'brigade'. My directions were vague, it was dark, and I was in a place I'd never seen before so I had a task in front of me. I could speak no French, so it was impossible for me to ask the way. I can remember going into many places, and had almost given up hope of finding my objective, when I was challenged by a sentry, who proved to be the brigade guard. This was the first real challenge I'd had under actual war conditions, and I thought afterwards, that the least hesitation in replying, on my part, might have meant a bullet, for it was reckoned at the front, that it was wise to 'shoot first and ask questions last'. My messages delivered, I made my way back to the camp in the field. Amongst our hastily erected bivouacs all was silent and everybody seemed to be sleeping; we'd had a hard and almost continuous trek from the coast, and were all very tired.

As I passed through the gate into the field, a bombardment opened up in front, and I stood and watched the flashes of the big guns. It was a grand, magnificent, and at the same time, an awe-inspiring spectacle to watch in the darkness. Great red jagged flashes played along the horizon, lighting up the sky with a lurid glare, while the 'boom, boom' of heavy artillery thundered through the night in a ceaseless cannonade. Well I knew, that every roar and flash carried with them death and destruction to those who were holding the line in the distance.

The following day was Sunday, and with it, came Church Parade. A Communion Service was held in the garden of the chateau being used as brigade hq, and Charlie Hutchinson and I attended. Excepting ourselves, the small party of communicants was composed of officers, including the Brig. Gen., so we were in high society that day. The afternoon was spent in improving our crude shelters. These as usual were formed from our waterproof ground-sheets, but we had already found an advantage in placing two or three sheets together, this giving us more space inside. We had no bedding of course; just the green turf of the field to lie on. After various inspections, we received our first pay in France – 5 Francs valued at ⅜, then. It was now quite apparent that our next move would be to the trenches, and we were still eager to be there, just as ready as when we were swinging along the green lanes of old England. On July 20th we had a route march as far as Bruay, which we found was a very dirty colliery village. Later in the day I had a run with despatches to Noeux-les-Mines, (the New Mines) and returned with exciting and all important news for the regiment.

11
Into the fighting line

That same night our 'A' and 'B' companies left the camp for the front line trenches. 'C' and 'D' left behind, envied them the honour of going in first, but wished them luck as they marched quietly away. They were to be in the line 48 hours, and then we of the other two companies would relieve them. In preparation for this the remainder of the battn. moved forward, the following day, to Labruie, a mining village in range of enemy guns, so at last we were under fire. On July 22nd we left Labruie for the trenches, passing en route the villages of Vaudricourt and Noeux-les-Mines, and, after darkness had fallen we reached the shell-shattered ruins of Philosophe, where we entered the communication trenches.

These were trenches leading up to the front line, and were constructed to give greater safety to troops approaching the fighting

line. We had already marched 13 miles, and now had 2 miles of
trench to struggle along in the darkness, in single file. It was, as
may be imagined, a rough and fatiguing journey encumbered as
we were with our full equipments. We were constantly becoming
entangled in wire or tripping and falling, now bumping one thing
and then another, whilst amid all the inevitable swearing and
grousing, there came hissing whispers to 'make less noise there'. It
was 1am as, almost exhausted, we at last came to the front line. The
relieved men slipped quietly away after telling us that all was quiet.
I had drunk all the water I carried, on the way (against orders of
course) and was glad when it began to rain. I set my canteen to
catch the rain drops and a wet night was never so welcome as that
one to me. During the night we took our turns doing sentry duty
in the fire-bays of the trench, and when relieved, we tried to rest
leaning against the parapet. There were no shelters or dugouts for
us. The Germans must have had an anxious time that night, and
I'm sure they would keep well under cover, as we kept up an
almost ceaseless rifle fire, which was perhaps quite unnecessary,
but then it was our first night in the fighting line. When morning
dawned we were in a terrible mess. The rain, mixing with the
chalky nature of the ground had made everything sticky, and we
had the appearance of being partly-white-washed. We received a
mouthful of tea at breakfast time, and a little stew for dinner made
at our camp kitchens in 'Quality Street' (Quality Street had been,
in pre-war days, a respectable group of dwelling houses; now it was
a heap of ruins – nothing more.) During the day we had the usual
exchange of artillery fire and trench mortars, but on our side at
least, there was little damage done and no casualties. After a really
uneventful 48 hours we left the trenches, being relieved by men of
the 7th K.O.S. Borderers, and marched back to Labruie. It was a
good long walk back after being in the line and the men were
about played out, and ready for a sleep. The same day we heard
rumours of an intended German attack, and at night we again left
for the line. However, we found things had returned to normal,
and instead of the trenches we went into billets in Marocq; known

as the 'Garden City'. This village of semi-detached houses had been the residence of middle-class people, and, in pre-war days, must have presented a very comfortable appearance. The inhabitants, however, as in many similar instances had been forced to flee for safety on the approach of the Germans, and their homes had been left with most of their splendid furnishings still in the rooms. Many houses were, of course, wrecked already from the effects of artillery fire. Marocq was quite close to the front line, but made a good though risky billet for us. We had been attached to the 145th London Brigade for purposes of instruction in trench warfare, and on July 26th I had orders to report to that Bde Hqrs, as cycle orderly, and so for a few days was separated from my old companions. During that time I had very little to do, and no one troubled me very much. It was during one of my daily journeys between Bde and Battn that I met a party of W. & C. Yeomanry and on enquiry found they were attached to our (15th) division. Although they were all strangers to me, it was interesting to meet men from the same district as myself, and they were able to give me news of a few of my own friends.

The days passed very quickly, and on August 2nd I rejoined the Camerons, while the following day we left our billets in Marocq and marched via Les Brebis and Mazingarbe to Vermelles, a little to the left of our recent position. This village had been the scene of very severe hand-to-hand fighting between French and Germans in the earlier days of the war, and now presented an awful wreckage of shell-shattered buildings.

The Camerons relieved the 8th Post Office Rifles, a London regiment, and we cyclists with the signallers were billeted in the village school. We were now battalion in support, and were therefore always ready for any emergency. On the 6th our billets were heavily shelled and we lost 1 killed (C.S.M. John Campbell of 'A' Coy) and 3 men wounded. These were our first casualties and the occurrence cast a gloom over the battalion. Sgt Major Campbell was an old soldier who rejoined for the war, and came from Egypt specially to join his old regiment. That afternoon I went to our transport lines at Hoochin, and brought back mails for the battalion. For a long time this continued to be one of my daily tasks, until I became well known as 'the postman', and was always eagerly welcomed on my return each day with my 'mail-bag', for letters and parcels were the great connecting link between us soldiers and home. Often I had to go through heavy shelling, at other times it was quiet, but I enjoyed the run out into the country behind the lines. It was a change from the cramped life of the trenches. We cyclists had many exciting adventures on our bikes carrying messages, bringing ambulances for wounded, and guiding officers here and there. We were looked upon as a sort of encyclopaedia of the district, and supposed to know where everyone and every place of importance was for miles around. There were, in fact, few places in the Loos sector that we did not know. We were relieved on the 18th August by the 7th Camerons and went out of the line to billets in Mazingarbe.

Next day we marched to Les Brebis for baths in the steam condensers of the mines. These condensers made excellent baths and we enjoyed them immensely. Nothing of much importance happened these days. I was kept busy with the usual despatch work and one day had a long run to the West Riding Clearing Hospital for a set of bag-pipes. This was a nice trip, which took me back beyond the town of Lillers. An incident happened at this time, which makes me smile yet when I think of it. Lt Cameron, my officer, sent for me one morning and said 'Look here Jackson, I want you to go to Bethune, and get me some things. You can speak French' (I hardly knew a word) 'and you'll manage fine'. Of course I couldn't argue; he was my officer, so off I set with 80 frs in my pocket. I got what was required by the simple but effective method of bringing the shopkeepers on to the street, and showing them the articles I wanted in the windows, returning to billets with a collapsible canvas bath, some scented soap, shirts and a pair of braces, and a large assortment of fruit. The officer laughed when I delivered my parcels, and complimented me on the success of my shopping expedition. We went into the trenches again on the night of August 30th. Night time was always chosen for relieving, darkness perhaps hiding many of the blunders that were made. After a quiet occupation of the trenches for some days, we came out into billets in Noeux-les-Mines for one night, leaving again in the morning for Labruveiere. Here we were clear of the fighting, and enjoyed a few day's rest in this country village, as divisional reserve. As things were quiet, Jack Stuart, another cyclist, and I, went for a long run round by the villages of Lapugnay, and Marles-Callon, to the town of Pernes. Here, we were in the French lines and we turned back in case we got arrested as spies We saw men of many French Colonial Regiments, including Algerians, Zouaves, and Spahis, dressed in their strange, brightly coloured uniforms, with short jackets and baggy trousers. Compared to our own drab uniforms they presented a gorgeous appearance. Sept 19, 20 and 21 were notable for heavy bombardments along the British front, and the continued dull boom of guns gave us lots to think about, for we were now on the eve of the battle of Loos. The battalion left Labruviere on the 23rd and in the midst of a violent thunder-storm, we marched to Drouvain, where instead of getting billets as expected, we were turned into a field for the night. What with the storm and the mud on the roads, we were all in a miserable state. Stuart, Rutherford and I sought refuge in a cottage where the woman of the house allowed us to sleep in an attic. It contained lots of straw and onions, but was much more comfortable than the wet field, and we were glad to have dry quarters to sleep in. All night the guns kept roaring and the shells went screaming and whistling through the darkness.

12

The battle of Loos

Saturday, 25th September 1915, stands out very prominently in the history of the glorious 15th division, till then untried in a real battle. On that date the eager, well trained young men, who enlisted in the early days of the war, gave an account of themselves hardly equalled in any engagement during the whole campaign. For days, previous to the 25th, the whole of the Loos sector had been under a state of continuous bombardment from our artillery, such a bombardment as had never been known before. This continued shelling of the enemy positions was necessary to destroy the enormous barbed-wire defences with which the German lines were protected. It also served the purpose of 'putting the wind up' our 'friends the enemy' across that narrow stretch of wilderness that separated us, and was known as 'No Mans Land'. For some time we had believed there was to be a great attack on this part of the front, and prided ourselves on the fact, that at last we should have the chance we had waited so long for, as the 15th division was to lead the attack. The 24th saw us preparing for battle. We were served out with 'iron rations' – hard biscuits, a tin of bully-beef, and a small tin of tea and sugar. Also we received a plentiful supply of ammunition, so that every man carried no less than 250 rounds, which was no light weight to be carting about. We were asked to destroy all letters and papers which might identify us in the event of us being taken prisoner. We were also advised to make out our wills in the space provided in our pay-books, which were then collected and stored away. All finally completed, the battalion moved forward to Philosophe, close to the front line trenches. Instead of going to rest for a few hours in the usual manner, we gathered in groups talking over our chances in the morning. Then the absolute coolness of everyone was shown by the fact that we commenced singing. All the old favourites were sung one by one, bringing back memories of training days, and old scenes of sunny, southern, England. Then friends wished each other 'Good luck', friends who knew that the next day would find many of them among the casualty list. Before dawn we began our journey to the trenches by way of Chapel Alley and Devon Lane. Our progress up the communication trenches was very slow. The air was full of the stifling odour of powder and gas, and once we halted to don our gas masks, reaching the firing line shortly before 5am.

Here I will give a description of our dispositions and various objectives. The attack was being made by the 4th Army Corps under the command of Gen Rawlinson. The left position was occupied by the 1st Division; men of the 'Old Contemptibles', whose objective was the strongly fortified Hohenzollern Redoubt. On the right was our old friend the 49th Division of London Territorials, a fine fighting force, who were to take the line on the right of the village of Loos. We (the 15th Scottish Division) had the post of honour in the centre, our goal being the village of Loos, and beyond that the now famous 'Hill 70'. The sector was of course familiar to us, and for a long time we had daily watched the shelling of the village, and its familiar steel tower at the pit-head, which was a land-mark for miles around. We were expected to take the village in about 3 days, and our reinforcements had been arranged for on that allowance of time. It was to be a hard struggle, but surely the general staff must have under-rated the dash and determination of the regiments engaged. Had reserves been lying near, Loos would without a doubt, have been a deciding battle.

At 5 o'clock after gas had been discharged against the enemy, and which through contrary winds was blown back and killed many of our own men, we mounted the parapet of the trench with the aid of short ladders, and so at last we 'were over the top'.

In 'no man's land' we found ourselves in a heavy mist, through which came the whirr and whine of shells and bullets. Men began to fall immediately, and one of the first to be killed was our signal officer, Lt Cameron, shot through the heart as he clambered out of the trenches. In short rushes we kept on, grim and determined, through a tangled growth of long grass, till we came to the enemy front line. With fierce yells, we were among the 'Jerries' and then ensued some terrible hand-to-hand fighting, as we showed them the art of using bayonets. Cutting, smashing, thrusting, we drove them before us to their second line, but even here they could not keep us back. True, they fought hard, but could not stand against our determination, and our terrible bayonets. In spite of growing losses in our own ranks we kept on driving the Germans before us and soon had them on the run for the village, and here they set up a desperate defence. Their machine-guns took a terrible toll from our thinning ranks, but still we hung on till we were again in hand-to-hand conflict with them. From house to house, and cellar to cellar, we hunted them. Machine-gunners slaying us from their hidden posts, threw up their hands crying 'Kamerad', when we got within striking distance, but these deserved and received no quarter. Cold steel and bombs did their duty then, and the village was strewn with dead and running with blood. Hundreds of prisoners, we had taken in the open, were sent to the prison camps in the rear of our lines, and at 8 o'clock in the morning we were in possession of the village. In 3 hours we had accomplished what had been planned for us to do in 3 days. As is always the case in a big battle, there had been a great mix-up of men and regiments, and now as we tried to re-organise for a further attack, men were placed under the nearest available officer irrespective of what regiment they belonged.

Our colonel – Douglas-Hamilton – was still with us, and also our adjutant, Capt Milne, a cool officer belonging the Indian Army.

Arrangements were now made to push on with the advance on 'Hill 70'. Meanwhile on our left the 1st Division was held up owing to the strong defences protecting the Hohenzollern Redoubt, so that we were suffering heavily from enfilade fire. On our right the 49th Division was keeping well up with us. Included in that division were the London Irish, who are credited with coolly dribbling a football in front of them as they advanced. Our own division had done well in gaining so much ground, though we had paid dearly for our success. Looking behind we could see artillery galloping forward in the face of a murderous fire, men and horses and guns being smashed up in strange-looking heaps. Our progress towards Hill 70 was slow, and we had to suffer terrible losses from that terrible cross fire from the Redoubt, which caught us on the left flank. It was unfortunate indeed that the 1st Div. were held up. Machine-gun bullets mowed down the long grass and weeds in which we lay, as a scythe cuts down corn in a harvest-field, and men on all sides were losing their life blood on that gently rising slope. So far I was unharmed, which seemed a wonderful thing to me. After a time we gathered together and charged the hill. A short fight and we had reached the top, held it for a time and were driven back by weight of numbers. Again we charged, held the top and were forced back. The situation was serious, and anxiously we looked back for reinforcements but no help could we see. A third time we charged on that awful hill-side, but the enemy with his reserves at hand, were too many for us and again we fell back. Truly we were holding to the motto of the regiment 'A Cameron never can yield'. We numbered at this stage less than 100 all told, and for all we knew might be all that was left of the 6th Camerons. As the evening drew near we made a fourth and final attempt to win and hold the ridge. This time we meant to do or die. Led by our brave old colonel, bareheaded and with no other weapon than his walking stick, we made for the top of 'Hill 70', through a murderous rifle and machine-gun fire, while shells crashed all around us. Our action was a sort of last desperate chance, but in the face of such heavy odds it could only end in failure. The white-haired old man who led us was shot dead, and shortly afterwards Capt Milne, cool and unruffled to the last, paid a similar penalty. Driven back to the foot of the slope as darkness came on we dug ourselves in, wondering what was happening around us. We had seen no sign of reinforcements, and now with the darkness came rain which made our position miserable. All day we had been struggling and fighting, and were glad of the chance to eat a biscuit as we lay in our shallow holes through that awful night, soaking wet and under a never ending fire from the enemy. Except from cuts and bruises from barbed wire, and the rough and tumble of the battle, I was still alright though separated from most of my companions, many of whom were wounded or killed. Sunday 26th was a day of heavy shelling along the British front. We made no more attacks, but hung on desperately to our new line and the ground we had gained.

Reinforcements had been hurried forward to support us, but these, men of the 21st Div. had never been in action before, but surely that could be no excuse for the poor fight they made. In many cases officers had to keep them in the trenches at the point of their revolvers, but even then were not always successful in their efforts. It seems a hard thing to say against a British division, and yet only a few weeks later this same 21st division made a great name for themselves on the very ground where they had failed us so badly. Throughout the day, in the mist and smoke of battle, we lay in our shallow holes with bullets whistling in all directions, with shells dropping and ploughing up the ground everywhere, and men being killed and wounded constantly. We'd had no decent meal since Friday night, and were parched with thirst, but still we kept a vigilant eye in front for the counter-attack that was sure to come. Late at night after all hope of any help seemed to have gone, we were relieved by the Guards Division, and never was relief more welcome. Battered, broken, and weary, we struggled back to the village of Mazingarbe, in little groups as best we could. So far we knew nothing as to what extent the battalion had lost in numbers, but I thought there could be few men left. It had been a fight such as the division had always wished for, and we had left our mark on the Germans. They would not forget the men in kilts in a hurry. The battle of Loos has been mentioned as the 'Camerons' day out' for there were no less than 5 battalions of the regiment engaged – the 1st, 4th, 5th, 6th and 7th. For his bravery on 'Hill 70' Col Douglas-Hamilton was posthumously awarded theVC, and I well remember the pride we all felt when the news became known. Had he survived I feel sure he'd have been as proud of his regiment, and the fight it made, as we were of his honour. In all, the division gained 6 VCs that day, besides many smaller distinctions. It was on the Saturday morning that Piper Laidlaw of the 7th Kings Own Scottish Borderers strode along the parapet of the trenches playing the battalion into action. On the 27th after we were rested and cleaned we had a battalion roll-call, one of the most touching scenes that can be imagined. What a little band we seemed to be, in place of the fine regiment of three days ago, as we gathered in the garden behind headquarters. Our Regimental Sgt Major, Peter Scotland, began calling the roll, company by company. There were few responses as names were called, though what little information there was about missing men was given by friends. All my friends of the cycle section had come through safely; Charlie Hutchinson and Andrew Johnstone were among the missing, but they eventually turned up slightly wounded. Another good friend, big 'Jock' Anderson was missing, and to this day his fate remains an unsolved mystery, but I have no doubt he did his bit, for Jock was a whole-hearted fighter. The losses of the division ran into thousands and our own battalion had lost 700 out of 950 who went into action. Of the whole forces engaged, the casualties for the week-end totalled over 69,000 officers and men.

The battle-field presented a wrecked and battered appearance. Dead men and horses lay everywhere, with smashed guns and wagons piled up in confusion. On the Vermelles–Loos road a whole supply column, caught by enemy artillery, had been smashed to pieces. From the broken barbed-wire defences streamed pieces of tartan and khaki, torn from kilts and tunics, as men had crashed through the entanglements when charging the enemy trenches.

A story is told in connection with the battle, of a Gordon Highlander, who, making his way back wounded from the fight, with bandaged head and arm in a sling, his kilt and hose all torn and bloody, came across a trooper of the Mounted Police standing in the shelter of the old church at Vermelles. As the wounded man slowly made his way past, the M.P., while he gazed at the wounds, the dirt and trickling blood of the 'kiltie', said in a condescending manner – '*Some* fight Jock!' 'Aye', said the Gordon, taking the cigarette from his lips, as he eyed the other up and down, from the red band on his hat to the polished boots and spurs on his feet, – 'and *some* don't'. On the 28th while fighting still continued near 'Hill 70' we left Mazingarbe and marched back to Hallicourt, bivouacking in a field near the village, during a night of heavy and continuous rain. On the following day we moved further back to the larger village of Labouissere, where we billeted in a barn and were fairly comfortable. For a day or two we had an easy time, and during our stay we were visited by the Corps Commander, Sir Henry Rawlinson, who came to congratulate us on our behaviour in our first battle. We also had an inspection and were addressed in satisfied terms by our divisional commander, General McCracken, who no doubt felt proud of his men. On October 3rd, we left Labouissere, and, passing through the large mining village of Marles we reached Allouagne. Here we were joined by a draft of reinforcements, and were glad to recognise many old friends amongst them; men who had been slightly wounded at Loos and were now returning to us from the Base. We spent a few quiet days in the little country village, while we were being refitted with uniforms and equipments, and our time was passed in light exercises. In spite of the horrors we had passed through in the great battle, we began to pick up again our jaunty devil-may-care ways. This was well, for soon we would be on our way back to the front line trenches, where it did not do to be depressed, and on October 12th we left Allouagne and marched to Hallicourt.

13

Some trench fighting

During our sojourn at Hallicourt, we were under half-an-hour's notice to move into the front line, and consequently were always on the *qui vive*. There was still heavy fighting in the region of Loos, and day by day the guns were sullenly booming in front of us. On the 15th we moved forward again to familiar quarters in the ruined village of Mazingarbe, where we patiently waited, knowing that any minute might find us on our way to the trenches. Towards night-fall the Germans made an attack, and the battalion left in a hurry for the front line, where we relieved the 8th London Fusiliers. Our front line was now the old German front line, and we had fairly comfortable quarters, when not actually on guard or working, in the marvellously constructed dug-outs that had been built by the enemy. Until now we had never been in such excellent dug-outs as these, our own shelters having been simple, cupboard-like recesses cut in the side of the trench. But these of the Germans were splendidly constructed and well underground. They were reached by a sort of stairway, in many cases having as far as 40 steps, and each had two entrances, at the extreme ends, to provide as far as possible, against being blocked in by the effects of shell-fire. We had an uneventful spell, save that at times the guns burst forth with renewed vigour and artillery duels waxed fast and furious. Generally speaking the days were a constant round of sentry go, trench maintenance and patrols in 'no man's land' after dark, coupled with the erection of barbed-wire entanglements as a defence against surprise attack.

On one of these days I had one of those little adventures which livened things up for us, and gave us cause to remember we were still fighting Germans. We were in the habit, on quiet days, of slipping down to the villages behind the lines for bread and eggs, or any eatables we could manage to buy from the villagers, who, in some cases, and in spite of the death and destruction which

surrounded them, still clung to their homes. This particular afternoon, Gibson, corporal of the signal section, and I thought we'd
take a walk to Philosophe for bread etc. As things seemed very
quiet we got out at the rear of the trench, with the intention of
going down the Loos–Vermelles road which crossed our lines a
little to our right. Hardly had we reached the road when three
shells dropped dangerously near us. 'Jerry' had evidently spotted us,
and we required no further warning to get back to the trench.
However, we went by the safer route of the communication
trenches, got our supplies, and decided to try the road for the
return journey as it was then getting dark. All went well for some
distance, when suddenly we heard the 'ping' 'ping' of bullets and 5
of them passed much too close to our heads to be pleasant. In an
instant we were down flat on our stomachs on the road, and were
wondering how we could get clear of the 'sniper', when we were
hailed by a Royal Scot from a neighbouring trench, who had
noticed us, and who informed us that if we crawled up the road for
a hundred yards we should be out of view of the sniper, so we
wormed our way up the road for some distance, but it was a relief
when we could stand up again, and finish our journey on foot. One
would expect such adventures would make us frightened; instead
we laughed over our hairbreadth escapes, it was all in the day's
work, so to speak. I remember one night after being relieved in that
same sector, four of us decided to wait till daylight before going
down to billets, so we all crawled into a dug-out that was half full
of ammunition: trench mortar shells, rifle grenades, bombs,
and hundreds of rounds of bullets. In the middle of this lovely
collection of explosives, we made a small fire, and had some tea,
afterwards calmly going to sleep while shells dropped continually
around us. What would have happened, had anything struck the
ammunition on which we lay, was a point of view, which worried
us but little. We were only four weary soldiers in need of a sleep.
Every day seemed to have its own little adventure. On October
24th, chancing to look over the parados to the rear of our lines, I
saw the body of a man lying about 50 yards behind the trench we

occupied. When darkness came on I went over to see if I could find out who it was. It was a sickening business going through his pockets for something to identify him. His face, as I found by the faint light of the rising moon, had been struck by a piece of shell and was a horrible sight, and the body seemed to have been lying for some time. After I had told my mates we went over again, and when all was quiet, we buried him in a shell-hole, almost lying beside the corpse ourselves as we covered him up as well as we could, our only light being the glimmering moon, and an occasional 'star shell'. Surely no man had a more 'eerie' burial. We worked silently like ghosts and our final service to the dead man was the erection of a simple wooden cross. From his papers, we found that he was Pte. C. Adie, 6th Royal West Kents, and a native of Tunbridge Wells. We sent a letter to his mother containing the sad news, and enclosing her own last letter to him. In return, we received a note thanking us for the little we'd been able to do for her son, and explaining that he had been posted as missing for 6 weeks. On the 26th, I was buried myself, only I happened to be alive and came up smiling once more. At this time Hqrs, were situated in two old German dug-outs, and so very near to the enemy lines, that we had strict orders not to show ourselves. All had gone well till the day we were due to be relieved by our sister battalion the 7th Camerons. Enemy observers must have noticed that something unusual was taking place, for in the afternoon, we were subjected to a steady bombardment. Only one gun seemed to be in use, but shells fell as regularly as the tick of a clock, and we soon realised that the deliberate, and methodical gun-fire was intended exclusively for our two dug-outs, and that we were caught like rats in a trap. First on one side, then on the other, those shells dropped around us and we wondered how long it would be before the German gunners succeeded in making a direct hit. At last with a dull thud a shell landed so near that we felt the dug-out crumple up, and in an instant all was darkness. There were four us of in that little shelter of earth; Jimmy Lawson, Jack Baird, Bob Muir, and myself. Lawson alone showed any fright while after the first shock I laughed, and the three of them today, would tell you that I began to whistle the regimental march. I asked 'anybody hurt', and found there were no casualties, so I said 'Cheer up, we have our trenching tools, we'll soon be out of here'. Directly we had been 'wrecked', the German gun had ceased fire, the observer evidently being satisfied that we could not have escaped being killed. As we were not deeply buried, it did not take us long to cut a way out through the soft soil. All this time we had wondered why none of the fellows, from the larger dug-out, a little distance away, had not come to our assistance, and we were greatly surprised to find that they had also been buried, but, like us, they had escaped injuries, except for one who had struck his head against an iron girder. What lucky lads we were. Fourteen buried and all alive and kicking at the end of the funeral. As the day changed to the grey light of evening, we dug out as much of the signalling apparatus, as we could find, under the persistent attentions of a sniper who luckily did us no damage, and we were all glad, and relieved in more senses than one, when we got clear of the trenches that night. We returned to poor billets in Noeux-les-Mines, where we had some very miserable weather. While here, a detachment 200 strong went to the village of Drowain for inspection by the King. Here also, we had our first meeting with the 1st Battn Cameron Hrs, in which of course we were greatly interested, they being a part of the famous 'Old Contemptibles', who had seen much fighting since leaving Edinburgh Castle in August 1914. On Nov 1st, our short respite came to an end, and again we moved into the trenches, relieving the 8th K.O.S. Bdrs. During this spell in the line I experienced the agonising tortures of thirst, from which a party of us suffered so much, that we tried to drink the drippings, that came through the roof. This was as black as ink, with equally as bitter a taste, which only served to increase our thirst, and accentuate our sufferings. We had been posted to an out of the way dug-out, and somehow were left without our daily supply of rations. Our position will be more easily understood, if I quote from my diary:

Nov 1st: Left Noeux-les-Mines at 9.30pm. Heavy rain.
                Took over from 8th K.O.S.Borderer's. 12 midnight.
                No rations arrived. Water finished.

Nov 2nd: Still raining. Much shelling both ways. Still no
                rations or water. Feeling very bad with thirst.

Nov 3rd: More rain and more shells. No rations, no water.
                Party in sore distress. Volunteered to go for water
                and something to eat. Fit again after a feed.

This will indicate our plight. On the third night Cpl Gibson and I went to hunt for rations, and I can picture us struggling along those trenches up by the waists in mud and water. In our weak state, it took us over 2 hours to go about 2 miles and we were absolutely done when we found the signallers' dug-out at Hqrs. Here we received some hot tea, than which, nothing ever was so acceptable or refreshing. A snack of food and a little rest put new life into us, and with water and as many rations as we could carry, we waded through those terrible trenches to our comrades, who were indeed glad to see us safely back, with food and water. For the whole of this spell the trenches remained in an awful state, due to the bad weather, and we were glad to get out on the 7th, and march back to good billets in a chateau at Noyelles, on the road to Bethune. Three days rest, and in we went again relieving the Royal Scots. The following day we lost 2 Sgts and 2 men killed, and 4 men wounded. We were again relieved by the Royal Scots on the night of the 13th Nov, and went down to old quarters in Noeux-les-Mines. Here, we had a few days of quietness, while we cleaned ourselves and equipments up again. On the 19th, we moved forward to Philosophe, and early on the 21st, we entered the front line, and relieved the Argylls. During this term in the trenches, a very curious accident occurred to two brothers named Hedspith. They were cleaning their rifles in the ordinary way after 'stand down' in the morning, when in some way their weapons were discharged, resulting in one being killed, and the other wounded. At the enquiry a verdict of 'accidentally shot' was given, but we never heard any details concerning the mystery. On the 24th, we were relieved by the 1st Northamptons, of the 1st Division, and while 'A' and 'B' Coys went to Philosophe, 'C' and 'D' took over the support trenches at Curly Crescent. On the 30th, we were relieved by the Royal Scots, and went to Noyelles. Here, in view of the fierce winter weather, we were issued with skin coats, seemingly like goat skins, and a funny lot we looked when arrayed in our 'fur coats' and kilts. On December 1st we marched still farther back via Sailly Labourse, Labourse, Verquigneiull and Verquin to the village of Vaudricourt. The weather continued to be very stormy, and we shivered to think of the poor fellows in the line, and at the same time we were glad to be able ourselves to lie snug in a barn at night, far from the firing line. After a few days here, all too short we thought of course, we moved forward again to Sailly Labourse, and here we found a large 'Soldiers Home' had been erected, wherein we were able to purchase many little luxuries, we hadn't seen for months. Another short turn in the line, and the battalion returned again to Sailly Labourse.

14

15th Division in rest

There were rumours of a month's rest, and the regiment needed it. The whole division was battle weary. On the 15th Dec we were relieved by our old friends of the 47th Division, and at last we were off for a change, and looking forward to it just as we'd look for a holiday at home. The battalion, with the exception of the cyclists, went by rail to the town of Lillers. At this point, I took charge of the cyclists in place of L/Cpl Pender, and, mounted on our bikes, we took the cobbled road to Lillers by way of Beuvry, Bethune, and Chocques. This happened to be my birthday, and I was in possession of a very nice cake sent from home, so, halting for a rest, we called at an *estaminet*, or inn, by the roadside, and had quite a spree with the cake, and some wine. After a happy interval, we pushed on again to join the battn, and with the signallers, were billeted in a barn at the rear of a gentleman's house, which although far from being an ideal residence, was a welcome change from what we had been accustomed to in and near the trenches. We made the barn as clean, and comfortable, as possible. There was some good clean straw for bedding and we settled down for a month's rest. Lillers was, so far, the largest town we had visited since our arrival in France. Troops were constantly passing through it, on their way to and from the front, but being out of general gun-range was still intact, and therefore we came much in contact with the civilian population. I cannot say we were very much impressed either by the town or the people. They were not, speaking generally, of the cleanest type, by any means, and their main object in life just then, seemed to be to make as much money as possible, out of the 'soldat Anglais'. However, we got along not too badly while we stayed in the place, and were thankful to be able to stay there so long. Being in rather more settled quarters than usual, we got much better food, and better cooking facilities were available, so that, with little to do except light exercises and occasional marches, the weariness brought on by hard, continuous fighting soon wore off, and we became once more the gay devil-may-care regiment of our training days. On Dec 19th we were visited by Sir John French, during his farewell tour of the forces. From now onwards, our Comdr-in-Chief was to be Sir Douglas Haig. The streets of the old-fashioned town were lined with troops, who gave the departing general a hearty send-off.

The days were passing quietly enough, although there was much excitement about Xmas time. The mail from home was eagerly watched for, and we had a royal time with the various nice things sent out to us from our friends, so much so, that before we got through with all the good things, we were almost sick of seeing cakes, shortbread, sweets etc. We signallers spent a very jolly Hogmanay night. There were two very good violinists in the section, and we had carried a violin about with us ever since we left England. This was brought out for the occasion, our billet was transformed into a ballroom, illuminated by pieces of candle stuck against the walls, and long after it ought to have been 'lights out', the dancing, singing, and the merriment were kept going. I believe I was the only really sober man of the crowd, everybody was in a happy mood, and I remember having to hold up Willie Hamilton on his feet, while he played us an old favourite tune, 'Auld Robin Gray'. I think we danced and sang till exhausted and till the candles stuck against the wall, flickered out.

1916: On Sunday Jan 2nd, a grand dinner and social evening was given to the men of 'C' Coy, by the Captain and junior officers, in Lillers Theatre and was a great success. The first course was of course the Scotch favourite – Haggis, made specially for the occasion in Edinburgh. We had a lively gathering with plenty of liquid refreshment to help down the dinner, and music by the pipers. Toasts and speeches were naturally the outcome of such a splendid feast, and we all spent a happy time. The officers of the company dined with us, and for once army discipline was left out, and they met us as ordinary friends and gentlemen. For one brief moment there was silence while every man stood to 'attention', at the call of the captain, as a tribute to the memory of our late commanding officer Lt Col Douglas-Hamilton VC killed at the head of his battalion at Loos.

One day, a draft arrived from the base, most of the men having been light casualties at Loos, and among these I was glad to meet two old friends in Andrew Johnstone and Sam Nicholson. Old pals like these two, were welcomed back to the regiment, and we had, of course, to repeat our adventures over again, since September, for their benefit. Soon after this, our period of rest being nearly expired, we made preparations for our return to the fighting line, and, early on January 5th, we marched out of the town of Lillers, and passing through the villages of Ecquedecques, Auch-au-Bois and Ligny arrived at Bonny early in the afternoon, having covered a distance of 15 miles. The following day we practised some divisional operations. We had a particularly hard day of it, and I remember one of our orders while on the march was to keep 10 paces in rear of a detachment of artillery, and it took some doing too. During the day, we passed through the villages of Dennebroeuq and Addinthein. After completing our two days training we returned to Lillers, and it was during the long march back, a large sore developed on my right ankle, which became so bad, that I had to give up duty, and went to the doctor on the 9th. As the division was on the point of moving, I was sent to the 46th Field Ambulance, and so at last I had to leave the regiment. This troubled me greatly, as I did not wish to lose touch with my old friends. For a few days I had an easy time in hospital, and received every attention to my leg. I had also good plain food, and plenty of it. On Jan 14th the division moved into the fighting area once more, and the Field Ambulance went by motor to new quarters in Mazigarbe. My leg was so much improved by the 16th, that I was discharged from the hospital, and joined the battalion again in Noeux-les-Mines. I was glad to be back again among my own friends, and found we had relieved the first division in the same sector we had left before Xmas. I had again to visit the doctor on the 20th owing to my leg becoming so painful with marching, and on the same date the signal section left Noeux-les-Mines, and, after halting for dinner at Mazingarbe, went forward and took over from the 4th Suffolks, on the left of the Hulloch Road, while we cyclists took up a position in a cellar, near the church at Vermelles. We were now back to the danger zone, and again in the midst of flying shells and whistling bullets, by day and night. For a few days the Germans shelled Vermelles heavily, many nasty-looking shells landing quite near our billet. The enemy seemed to be smarting under the hammering he got from us at Loos, and was wrecking every build-ing, that might seem capable of sheltering men. On the 23rd, the Argylls came up and relieved us, and we went back to billets in Philosophe. It was one night during their spell in the trenches, that a patrol of the 8th Seaforths found the body of Col Douglas-Hamilton VC, which had lain out in 'no man's land', since he was killed in September. He was buried amongst many of his own men, in the military cemetery at Vermelles. For a day or two we had a quiet time, during which our equipments were examined, and our ammunition renewed. Most particular attention was paid to our gas helmets, as these at any moment might be the only means of saving our lives. The Germans were now using very deadly gas, and once they came at us with liquid-fire, but our rapid rifle-fire was much too good for them to face, and the liquid-fire attack came to nothing. We returned to the line, and relieved the Argylls on Jan 26th, the cyclists taking up a relay post for messages in Vermelles. The following day, I had the pleasure of seeing three 'Jerry' attacks repulsed. It happened to be the Kaiser's birthday, and no doubt his army wished to celebrate the event, but we were watching, and prepared for their sudden attack. Jack Stuart and I were making our way up the communication trenches, when we heard a great outburst of rifle fire. In an instant, we knew that the enemy was attacking so we climbed out of the trench, and on to the ruins of a house in order to get a view. On the left of the sector we occupied, the line was held by dismounted cavalry, who had not been in the trenches long, and it was against these newcomers that the Germans made their attack. In broad daylight we watched the lines of grey figures come over the top, getting riddled with bullets at every step, till they were about half-way across 'No Man's Land'. There, their ranks were broken, and they turned tail and made for their own trenches again. It was not long, however, before they came again, but their attack failed against concentrated rifle fire. Once again they tried to reach our lines, but again they were foiled, and they must have lost a few score men that afternoon. However, apparently not content with the lesson they had just received, the enemy shifted their attack to the right, and in the evening made another attempt against the 46th Brigade of our division. Here, they were up against the 10th H.L.I., and got more than they bargained for once more. Heavy artillery fire then commenced, and continued all night and next day. On this date (28th Jan) the enemy fired a mine under our front line, and we had

18 casualties. One man was extremely fortunate, being blown out of the trench, and for a distance of 30 yds over our barbed-wire defences into 'No Man's Land', from which position he crawled back under the wire, without having suffered any material injury. The Argylls relieved us on the 29th, and we in turn took over the reserve position from the Royal Scots. Next day, Sunday, Cpl Dunsyre VC Royal Scots, who gained his cross at Loos, and who was only recently returned from England, after being decorated by the King, was fatally wounded by a rifle-grenade. I saw him carried past on a trench board, wounded practically from head to feet, and in terrible agony. He died before his bearers could reach the dressing station. The following day while walking round the signalling stations, I was struck behind the ear by a small piece of shrapnel, but it did no more harm than draw blood. The 45th Brigade was relieved on February 1st by the 44th, our position being taken over by the 10th Gordon Highlanders, while we proceeded to billets in Mazingarbe. For a week, we were clear of the trenches, during which time some of our men went home on leave. 'Leave' was the burning question with us all at this time, and my own turn seemed to be getting near. One day I had a message to deliver at Noeux, where one of our signallers had charge of the divisional cinema. Poor Tulloch did very well as operator till the night he set the 'picture house' on fire, and so lost a very 'cushy' job. Things were fairly quiet with us in billets, though one night we had a sudden call to arms and 'stood to' in readiness for a quick move forward, which never came off. Another day, 'Jerry' dropped two shells in the village killing 6 and wounding 16 men. Monday, 7th Feb found us in action again, and this time the regiment was posted in and around the village of Loos. I was left behind to look after Hqr rations, and was responsible for seeing them delivered in the front line each night. Besides food, I took forward the coke for use as fuel in the dug-outs and cellars. Last, but not the least important item, was the rum ration, a very desirable article to men who had to contend with severe winter weather. Every night at a variable time between 10 o'clock and midnight, the transport journeyed up the

Loos road. Sometimes all was quiet, but at any moment the rattling of wheels on the hard road might be heard by the enemy, and then the shelling commenced. There was one night just after we passed 'Quality Street', when the calmness of the night was suddenly broken, as an enemy battery opened fire on us, and half a dozen shells landed with a crash just across the road. A slightly lower elevation of the guns, and 'Jerry' would have wiped our transport column clean out. Such instances as this were all in the night's work for the transport men, and casualties among men and mules engaged in this work, were frequent. A few days later I was busy cleaning my cycle in Philosophe when a shell came whining overhead, and dropped just behind our billet. I though it a funny place for a shell to fall, so hearing another on the way I stepped to the corner of the house, curious to see where it would land. To my surprise it crashed through the house next to where I stood. This happened to be a billet occupied by the Gordon officers. For a little while after the crash, there was nothing to be seen but falling bricks, tiles, and clouds of dust. Then I espied an officer running for dear life dressed only in pyjamas, while close at his heels came a cook with a frying-pan in his hand. The situation was so comical that although I was in the midst of the flying debris, I had to laugh. Luckily, no one seemed to have been hurt. The battalion came out of the line on the 10th Feb and I had tea ready for the signallers on their arrival in billets. My leg had been again causing me much trouble, and though averse to giving in, I was forced to see the doctor, as I could hardly walk for pain. For two days, I tried to get fit again by the use of hot fomentations, but on Sunday 13th, the regiment being once more bound for the trenches, the doctor sent me to the 47th F. Ambulance. There my leg was dressed and I was sent on to the 45th F. A. at Noeux-les-Mines, where I was lucky enough to catch a convoy of ambulance cars, and in the afternoon I arrived at the West Riding Casualty Clearing Station, a hospital of marquees situated outside Lillers. Here, I had every care from British Red Cross nurses, and none but those who have passed through so much fighting know the feeling of comfort and pleasure caused by being looked after by British women, and these were the first I had seen for many months. My doctor was a very nice gentleman named Symons. A general day's routine in the hospital was as follows: 5.30am Washed, 7am Breakfast, 8.30am Doctors visit, 12.30pm Dinner, 4pm, Tea, 6.30pm Cup of cocoa, 8pm Bedtime, and Lights Out at 9pm. I was, of course able to get up, and move about the ward, and to assist those less fortunate than myself. We had books and papers to read, and a gramophone greatly helped to pass the weary hours for those unable to leave their beds. To me, the change from the constant days of danger, and fighting, seemed as from earth to heaven. My connection with the 6th Cameron Highlanders was broken, though as yet I did not realise it. I was hoping I'd get no further down the line, as I did not wish to leave my old friends. My thoughts were always with the regiment, and being 'out of action' was something I did not care much about. My leg was getting neither better nor worse, and I wondered how long it would be before I could rejoin the battalion. On the 18th the doctor ordered me to the Base Hospital. Even then, I could not think my days with the good old regiment were passed. So it proved however, and here I take my leave of my trusted friends of the 'Fighting Sixth'.

15
Through hospital to 'Blighty'

Early on the morning of February 19th I entrained, along with a large number of wounded from the W.R.C.C. Station, in a French Red Cross train at Lillers. Every man was in a happy mood as far as wounds would permit, for we were on the way to a base hospital, and perhaps later on some of us might get home to England. Now that I had really left the trenches I began to consider my own chances of 'Blighty', though in my case, it did seem very far away.

My leg appeared to be at a standstill, getting neither better nor worse, though at times I suffered much pain. From Lillers, the train ran down to Merville, where it took on board another detachment of wounded, then back again to St Venant, Lillers, Chocques, past the mining village of Marles, through Frevent, Morgny, and down to the old town of Rouen. We passed through some very nice country during the journey, and just before entering Rouen the train came to a stand on the fine bridge over the Seine from which we obtained fine views of that famous river. Arrived at the station, after nearly 24 hours train journey, we were met by motor ambulances, and conveyed to No 1 Camp, where we were allotted to the various marquees of the hospital. After a bath and change, I was sent to bed to await the Doctor's inspection. The weather was bitterly cold, and heavy snow fell soon after our arrival, which made things worse than ever. I occupied the bed next the doorway, and it was pretty chilly lying there, as the tent was devoid of any fire or heating apparatus. Everything was kept clean and tidy, we were well fed, and received every attention from the nurses. Each morning at 3am the night nurse came along with hot water and towels, and we sat up in bed to wash. Breakfast was an early meal, R.A.M.C. men doing the serving. Then beds were made all ready for the doctor's visit, at which time we laid as still as if on parade. Daily, some of the wounded were marked 'Blighty', which meant home, and happiness for the fortunate ones, and made the remainder wonder if ever, and when, their turn would come. Most of my time was spent in reading papers, and writing letters, sometimes listening to yarns by other chaps, for each man had his own adventures to speak of. Although all kinds of dressings and ointments were used, my leg did not yield to any treatment, and I began to have hopes of getting home. I had now been in hospital three weeks and one morning the Dr shook his head, and said I puzzled him, 'in fact I think I'll send you to England' he said as he pulled out his pencil to write the all-important word 'Blighty' across my chart. Just then, the Sister asked him, had he tried such-and-such treatment, and back went the pencil into his pocket. My soaring hopes dropped to zero as he applied this new dressing. Next morning, the doctor, after doing his rounds went, as was his usual custom, to have a cup of tea with the Sister in charge of the ward, and as he was passing out again, he stopped suddenly at the doorway, turned about, and stepping to my bed, he marked me for home. The action was so unexpected, I hardly knew what to think. I had been writing a letter home, so I at once concluded it with the remark, 'When you receive this letter I'll be in England'. That afternoon, I went with many others to the docks and was put on board the Red Cross boat 'St Denis'. We slept aboard all night, some in cots and some on the floors. We sailed at 6.30 on the morning of March 6th and being a 'walking patient' I was allowed on deck. Everything was clean and comfortable, and R.A.M.C. men attended to the various needs of the wounded. The voyage up the Seine, beyond showing us some very pretty scenery, was uneventful and at noon we were off Havre. Out on the Channel I became very sea-sick, and wished the voyage over. At 5pm, we sighted the Isle of Wight and I'll never forget the excitement of one artillery-man, who had lost his speech through shell-shock. Seeing the English coast in the distance, he kissed his hand in that direction, then turning round he shook his clenched fist at the distant shore of France. Poor beggar, his dumb actions described his thoughts more accurately than any words could have done. The sight of England was pleasant to us all. Our escort of torpedo-boats left us, and we discarded the lifebelts we had worn while crossing the Channel. At 6.45pm we anchored in Southampton Water, and again slept on board over night. We took on our pilot at 8.30 in the morning, and berthed an hour later, disembarkation commencing at 10am.

Red Cross trains were in waiting, and soon we were dispatched to various parts of the country. I came via Basingstoke, Oxford, Birmingham, Crewe and Carlisle, where I was lucky enough to meet a friend on the platform, the officer in charge of the train, allowing me to leave it to speak to her. I had hoped we might go to hospitals in Carlisle, but instead we travelled north to Dundee, arriving there in the early hours of the morning. Here, we were distributed among various local hospitals, and I had the good luck to go to a small V.A.D. place at Monifieth. I had come from Rouen with a Cameron of the 7th Battalion, and by a coincidence we were now taken in hand by a 5th Cameron, who made a bath ready for us and arranged that we occupied the beds on each side of his own. We were ready for a good sleep and it felt fine to be safely back home. Of course, as the latest arrivals from the front, we had to answer numerous enquiries about the fighting in France. Hospital life, when one was able to get about as I did, was very enjoyable, especially when we were attended by nurses, who never tired of doing their best for us. We had a decent old doctor, who came every morning to see us, and after his visit, those who were well enough were allowed outside, but we generally assisted in cleaning out the ward first, dusting or polishing as required. There were also various indoor games, as well as a gramophone to amuse us, while as another means of passing the time, we were taught metal and fancy work, wood-carving, basket-making, etc, the articles we made being readily bought by visitors to the hospital. Sometimes we were invited, in small parties, to tea and social evening in the vicinity. For those who were fit enough the golf links at Monifieth were free to us. I had one afternoon's golf, as a result of which, I was put back to bed with a temperature of 104°. No doubt this was due to over-exertion; at all events I played no more golf, but confined my exercises to quiet walks. I spent one pleasant afternoon as one of a party, invited for the afternoon, to Egmont Cottage, where we were entertained to tea by Mr & Mrs Edwards. At the Whist Drive in the evening I was lucky enough to win first prize, a pocket case which I keep as a memento of happy days at Monifieth. It is a curious thing that directly I went to Monifieth, my injured leg began to heal, and after three weeks in hospital I was feeling quite fit, and knew it would not be long till I received my discharge. Now that I had been so long away from my old companions in France, I was not anxious to leave hospital, but, although the doctor seemed reluctant to mark anyone 'out', I knew my turn must come. About the end of March, along with a New

Zealander named Luke, and Briddon of the Yorks and Lancs Regt, I went along to the Red Cross Hospital in Dundee, and received a new kit, excepting a kilt. In the evening we said 'Goodbye' to the matron, nurses and friends, and set off on ten days leave before reporting to the military authorities. I had a pleasant welcome home by old friends, and, being the first soldier home to my native village from active service, I had to give descriptions and details of life at the front to almost every one I met. Like all holidays, this one passed too soon, and one day I received the all-important orders from the Depot at Inverness to report to Stirling, which made me wonder what regiment I could be joining there. On April 10th, I left home, and journeyed north once more, and at Stirling I was directed to the village of Cambusbarron. On the way, I met Major Scott-Kerr, the officer with whom I had gone to France, and in the mills of Cambusbarron, I found the 8th Battalion Cameron Highlanders.

16

At Stirling

I was now attached to 'D' Coy of the 8th Camerons, that company being composed solely of 'Expeditionary Force' men. After getting rid of my kit, I strolled into the Y.M.C.A. Hut, which had been built for the use and comfort of the soldiers, and got the shock of my life, when I met, face to face, Malcolm Draper, of my own company in the 6th Battalion, who had been shot through the stomach, and left for dead at Loos, yet here he was playing billiards. Soon I met a number of old friends, all of whom I was glad to see again. Next morning, I was examined by the doctor, and thereafter became attached to the 'slow walking party', better known as the 'Charlie Chaplins', this for the reason that all had a limp, some real and some imaginary. I tried to cultivate a sort of trail-the-leg walk myself, just for appearance's sake. All that we did, was to take a walk – a very gentle walk, with plenty of halts, three times a day under a sergeant, also one of the lame variety. If we happened to meet an officer on the road, we were all 'very lame' of course. My leg was healed up, and only required a little massage to take away the stiffness.

With the exception of 'D' Company, all the men at Cambusbarron were recruits, and these were in various stages of training. Men who had been to the front were not so hard worked. It was not long till I was fit for ordinary training, and I was taken out of the 'slow party'; another step in the direction of France again. Under the command of Scott-Kerr, the battalion was well looked after. He believed in feeding his men, and we had both variety, and plenty of food, while he saw to that by making a personal inspection at meals every day. Soon after I arrived a signalling class was commenced, and I was asked to join, which I did. Knowing that a course of signalling would keep me out of a draft for some time, and it was easier work than the ordinary routine. In addition to the usual parades of the day, we had at times to do guard, and also fire-picket duty, otherwise our evenings were free, and we generally went down to Stirling or as far as Bannockburn for a walk. Good Friday was kept as a holiday except for Church Parade, at Holy Trinity, Stirling. Next day April 22nd, I was on duty as Battalion Orderly Cpl, having to supervise the correct drawing of rations from stores, attend guard mounting, and accompany the C.O. on his morning inspection. Altogether, I was enjoying life at Stirling very much.

Once or twice a week drafts were leaving for service overseas, recruits, who had passed through their training, going along with expeditionary force men, who had recovered from their wounds. These little detachments always had a great send off, the young, untried soldiers all happy in the excitement of going out to the front, those more experienced thinking soberly of what they had already passed through. About the end of April, during one of the periodical medical inspections by the doctor, I was once more marked 'fit for active service', but I was now in the middle of a course of signalling; the one thing that stood between me and the trenches. My luck was holding good and though for the time being I was safe enough, I knew that some day I must return to the fighting line. Having as a cyclist, been attached to the signalling section in my old battalion, I was fairly well acquainted with the duties of a signaller, and got on very well in the class under instruction. We were taught various methods of signalling, using flags, buzzer (telephone) and heliograph, also lamps for night work. We put in many days of hard and continuous work in the interesting art of signalling, and soon I was promoted to the senior class.

It was rarely that the class paraded with the battalion, the exceptions being route marches, or any special schemes. On May 2nd, we were all turned out for a route march, and had only got outside the village of Cambusbarron, when we were ordered back to barracks on account of a Zeppelin raid on the east coast. There was some unusual excitement, and pickets were out all night, but we happened to escape a visit from the Zepps. As time passed on, we got more advanced in our work as signallers, and it became necessary to carry out big schemes to test theories in practice. The district adjacent to Stirling was well adapted for the purpose, and these schemes were looked forward to by us all, as it meant a day among the hills, and we used to set off in gay spirits to take up our positions with our kits, and a days rations, along with us. Being a good cyclist, and used to map reading etc, I was often sent, before the schemes took place, with the Sgt to select the most suitable positions for signal stations, and spent many a nice outing while so engaged. On one occasion we succeeded in making communication between Stirling Castle and Dunfermline by flag and heliograph. I got very well acquainted with the country for miles around, and one could not wish to see more beautiful scenery than lies in a radius of 20 miles of Stirling. About this time I had a good pal in Tom Brace, a Welshman, and many a fine time we had together. We managed to become acquainted with the maids at a large house near to where we lay at Cambusbarron, and it often happened that we were invited to go and have supper, and spend the evening with them. The people of the house, too, often had our officers as visitors, and frequently while they enjoyed themselves in one part of the house, Brace and I were having as nice a time, perhaps nicer, than our gallant officers, with the maids in the kitchen. Saturday mornings always found us paraded in Kings Park, Stirling, dressed in our kilts in full marching order for skirmishing practice, this being our only parade for that day. The afternoons were free except to those on special duty, so that we often took the privilege of weekend passes, to visit surrounding towns. Once or twice I went home to Carlisle, returning early on Monday morning for duty at 9am. At intervals, I was detailed for duty at weekends as Battalion Orderly, and in that capacity had to accompany the 'C.O.' on his weekly inspection, which commenced at 12 noon on Saturdays. We began by a visit to the cook-house, and after inspection of other out-buildings none of which escaped a visit, we reached the dining-room, by which time dinner was being served. I used to take a pride in stepping into that room and yelling 'The whole – Shun – Commanding Officer – any complaints?' At the first command there was silence, everyone laying down their knives and forks. As the 'C.O.' passed by each table in turn, the senior man would rise and say, 'No complaints, Sir'. Very rarely was there a complaint made; we were well fed and knew it. From the dining-room we passed to the men's quarters where all had been left clean and neat. Then, the round of inspection over, I was free to go and have my own dinner. On June 13th, a memorial service to Lord Kitchener was held in South Parish Church, Stirling, attended by the whole regiment and also by our neighbours the 12th Gordons. With the long slow steps of the Dead March, we passed between crowds, down the narrow streets of the town to the church, where the pipers played the famous lament 'Lochaber no more'. The service concluded with the sounding of 'Last Post' by the buglers stationed outside, all ranks standing to 'attention' in silent respect to the memory of a great soldier. Signalling instruction was still going on, and one day I was sent, armed with maps and compass to examine and select signal stations for a large brigade scheme. During the scheme I had charge of a station on the Airth road, from which we had to get in touch with the Gordons, some miles distant, and also one of our own stations across the River Forth. Through some error of their own the Gordons never showed up at all, but we had good communications with the other Camerons until heavy mist came down and destroyed all visibility. Our station was complimented on a good day's work by Captain Fraser, Bde Sig. Offr who had been keeping an eye on us with a telescope. Shortly afterwards, our course of signalling came to an end, and we had to pass an efficiency test, which took two days to complete. In the end I passed out as 1st Class Signaller with 399 marks out of a possible 400, the next best being a particular friend of mine, L/C Jimmy Monteith with 396. We were now once more ready for the front, for like myself, Monteith was home from the trenches, and we might expect draft leave anytime. There had been preparations made for battalion sports, and many fancied runners were training in readiness, one especially, the previous year's winner of the half-mile, being coached by certain officers. I had entered for the 100 yards race for expeditionary men and did well to secure third place, the winner being that same Sgt, who won the 100 yards, at the great sports meeting of the 45th Brigade at Chisledon, in 1915. The next event, in which I took part, was the obstacle race, which I won easily by a quarter of the course. In the ¼ mile I gained second place, and immediately that race finished I returned to the starting post for the ½ mile. The officer in charge wished to delay that race in order to give me a rest, but I said I was ready anytime. This was my favourite distance, and although it was regarded by many as a foregone conclusion, that last year's winner would again prove successful, and for which purpose he had been specially trained, I was just as determined that this would be my race. I was more or less a 'dark horse', to all except a few of the old 6th, and they were wise enough to keep silent. Above all, only a short time ago, I had been a 'crock', one of the 'Charlie Chaplin' squad, 'how could I beat the favourite?' We ran a splendid race but their champion never could master me, and I won by yards. Our signal sergeant, himself a great runner came over, surprised and delighted, to offer congratulations, saying 'I never expected anything like that out of you'. I had often joked with the signallers and told them I'd show them how to run at the sports, but never thought I'd do so well among men who had never been out of the country. Then big Jim Smith the bombing instructor, and at one time my platoon sergeant, came to me and said, while he gave me a good hard slap, 'Good old 6th Battalion'. It was good to find the old hands still took a pride in the 6th Battalion.

That day of sport was plain proof that I was fit and well, and now I began to get general training in readiness for a draft. There was much practise in bombing, and bayonet fighting, and we put in some hard and tiring work. But if it was hard training, it was also interesting, and we had great fun among the dummy figures, representing 'Jerries' in trenches, on our training ground. As result of constant practice we became very proficient in the use of the rifle and fixed bayonet, but as the degree of proficiency in the art of using a bayonet might one day mean the difference between life and death for each of us, it was to our advantage to know all the tricks. At this time the Battle of the Somme had begun and drafts of men were constantly being despatched to the front, so that it was no surprise to find to find myself under orders for France again. Once more I went home on short leave which gave me the privilege of saying 'Good bye' to friends. A few days later I was back in Stirling ready for whatever might come. We understood our draft was to reinforce the 6th Battalion, and so I looked forward to meeting my old comrades of earlier days. Jimmy Monteith was also one of the draft, and as friends we decided to stick together as long as possible, and I remember that we exchanged addresses of friends, as we sat on the beach at Folkestone, whom we wished to be written to should anything serious happen to either of us.

17

Back to France

One evening, the draft was inspected by General Jamieson, and we left Stirling en-route for France. I remember well, the crowds of people in the station to see us off. There were the usual good wishes, a short, sad 'Good bye' between friends, and we left Stirling behind, with only the memories of a very happy time. At Dunfermline, we joined forces with a detachment of Black Watch, and from there we ran swiftly to the Waverly Station, Edinburgh. Here, we picked up a number of Gordon Highlanders, so that now there was a full train of us, all bound for the front. Most of the men were going out for the first time, and their excitement was just as evident, as when my own regiment left Swindon more than a year before. Here and there, one saw the man who had who had already been 'through it', easily known by the set lips and quiet composure with which he viewed the scene in the station. Near by stood the pipers of the Gordons playing stirring music, and concluding, as our train moved off, with the pleading tones of 'Will ye no' come back again?' Monteith and I settled ourselves for the long, hard journey before us, while at Newcastle I was glad to meet some friends, who handed us some welcome refreshments, at the same time wishing us luck and a safe return. Through the night, we rattled on towards London, and without halting there, we passed on to Folkestone, arriving at that port shortly before noon. Here, we were allotted some large empty houses on the sea front, in which to rest. There was no chance of getting out of this 'rest camp' to see round the town, so Jimmy and I went down and sat on the shore and talked and wondered how long it might be till we were safely back.

In the afternoon, we went aboard the SS 'London', and, after an uneventful passage, we reached Boulogne about 4.30pm. We were marched to a rest camp for the night, and once more found ourselves under canvas. Next morning, we took the train for

Etaples, and were placed in the lines of the 5th Camerons. This was a disappointment to me, as it seemed we should not get to the 6th Battalion as I had expected, and so in time it proved to be. After the usual medical, kit, and such like inspections, we paraded the following afternoon for the 'bull-ring'. The bull-ring was a large sandy tract of land about 2 miles from camp, on which all new drafts had to pass through the latest ideas in training before proceeding to join their respective units in the firing line. Under the supervision of a large number of Staff N.C.Os, many of whom took a delight in making things as hard as possible, we were put through our paces. I remember there was a very stiff course of obstacles on the bullring, and to find out just how good we were at it, the instructors put us over the course in a sort of competition, and as was only natural the men did their best for the honour of their respective regiments, because each man believes his own is the best regiment in the army. The four, representing the Camerons, beat the others nicely after a tiring race in the loose sand. Later we were tested in bayonet fighting, a few of us being picked out at random to oppose sergeants who were considered experts, and who, undoubtedly, were very smart at the game. A Staff Sgt Major took me in hand, perhaps thinking, as I wasn't very big, he'd have an easy time. He might have picked a bigger man and got a better time, because I could handle a rifle and bayonet then, and we were still hard at it when the rest were finished. His weapon was a long light stick padded at the end with sacking, mine a rifle and bayonet in scabbard. His aim was to beat my guard, and gain a 'hit' on my body or legs, while I was to act solely on the defensive. He found I could out-manoeuvre him, and he failed to hit me, but out of sheer bad sportsmanship he struck me between the eyes with his stick. It was lucky for him my bayonet was in the scabbard, or I could not have resisted giving him an inch of cold steel for the foul blow. Seeing all the other instructors standing near, he apologised for his hasty action, and owned that I had mastered him, and the incident closed with that, though it left me with a swollen eye and a bruised forehead. For a few days we put in a good of hard work in the bull-ring, hard wearing work for even the fittest of men. We did a fair amount of shooting at the Quarry Range, much trench digging, and bayonet exercises. In addition, we had lectures on various subjects in connection with the fighting line, also bombing attacks by night, which produced great fun. We were served out with the latest idea in gas-masks, and one day had to don our masks and pass through a long tunnel filled with poison gas, one breath of which would be sufficient to kill a man. It needed nerve to go through, and confidence in the mask was essential. I saw one poor fellow who cried when his turn came. The officer in charge coaxed him, but to no purpose, and it was not until the officer had gone through it in *his* mask that the man would go. We found, on enquiry, that he had previously been 'gassed' hence his fear of the gas-chamber. The weather was at this time very hot, and we had thunder-storms, which made a terrible mess of our tents. One day we had a 'washing parade' in the camp wash-house, when we washed all our dirty clothes. Another day, we marched to Paris-Plage for a bathe in the sea which was enjoyed immensely. There were various places of recreation in and near the camp, where we could spend our leisure time in the evenings. A large cinema was a great attraction, as were also the huts of the Church Army and Salvation Army. Directly opposite our lines, was the large hut maintained by Lady Angela Forbes and known to all the troops as 'Angelina's'. In it, we could purchase a nice tea or supper, served over the counter by English girls. Almost nightly, there were concerts at which any so gifted could step on the platform and sing, and many a fine time we had during the time we stayed at the 'base' camp.

My last night at Etaples was spent as Corporal of the Guard, and I remember a very laughable incident, in connection with the sentry outside. Everything was peaceful and still, when about midnight there rang out the quick challenge of the man on guard 'Halt, who goes there?' Listening carefully, I could hear the sound of approaching footsteps, and it seemed as if the challenge of the guard was being ignored. Another challenge by the sentry 'Halt, or

I fire', caused me to grab my rifle, and rush outside. Asking what was wrong, the sentry answered 'come and see, it's that damned "cuddy" of Angelina's'. We could do nothing but laugh. The noise of the donkey's feet on the hard road had seemed to be the steps of two men, and it did look comical to see him holding up the donkey at the point of the bayonet. As a gentle reminder to keep better hours, we gave it a cheerful prod in the ribs with the cold steel, which set him off at his best gallop down the road, and for some minutes we could hear nothing but the challenge of sentries on each side, but 'Neddy' answered to no one, and kept up full speed till out of our hearing. Before our turn of guard duty expired, I was hurried off to join a draft for the front, and so from the monotonous life of the base camp, I was soon to be in the thick of the fighting in the trenches. It was my chief concern to know if I'd join my old comrades, but from what we could learn it seemed we were bound for the 1st Camerons, which did not appeal to me at all, but I was glad to know that Jimmy Monteith was going along with the draft, so at least I was sure of having one good friend in the new regiment to which we would soon belong.

18

With the 1st Camerons

Entraining early in the afternoon, we left Etaples and proceeded eastwards towards the 'front'. By night time, we had reached Rome's Camp, and here we stayed all night. In the morning, we rejoined the train, and, passing through the town of Amiens, we reached Albert, round which was being fought the Battle of the Somme. The town was in ruins as the result of artillery bombardments, but presented a scene of great activity so far as troops were concerned. An object of interest, which caught the eye long before reaching the town, was the figure of the Virgin on the top of the Cathedral, which was also ruined by gun-fire. The figure of the Virgin Mary had been partly dislodged and hung in a dangerous position over the street, where it seemed as if at any minute it would come crashing down. We found the 1st Camerons out of the front line for a rest, and they seemed to be in need of one. They had had a rough time while on the Somme and were only 80 strong when we joined them, and were the most tired looking soldiers I ever saw. Monteith and I were lucky enough to be posted to the signal section, then under the command of Sgt Pollok, better known as 'Pip'. We found quite a number of 'Old Contemptibles' in the section, men who could and did talk of the landing of the expeditionary force, of the retreat from Mons and the battles of the Marne and Aisne. They seemed a devil-may-care lot, but welcomed us kindly. In the morning, under the Regt Sgt Major, Sydney Axton, known through all Cameron ranks as 'Old Joe', we paraded for inspection by the C.O. Colonel Craig-Brown. As a new draft, we had come out wearing khaki kilt aprons, and I well remember the first order of the R.S.M. was, 'Take of your aprons and show your Cameron tartan'. 'Old Joe' was the real old fashioned type of soldier, a smart man in every way, a terror for discipline when on duty, a thorough gentleman off duty. A man who would sing a song or dance with the best; who knew every-thing there is to know about soldiering, and took the greatest pride in his regiment. His decorations numbered 9, and included the Military Cross, won on the Aisne, and the Distinguished Conduct Medal, won during the South African war, so that he was a real old warrior. His word was law in the battalion, and he would give an officer a 'lecture' just the same as he would a private soldier, so that all ranks looked up to him as a man to be respected. Personally I always got on well with him, my duty bringing me often in contact with him, and I soon learned that his bark was much worse than his bite. I found out that my old regiment was lying quite near to the town of Albert, and took the opportunity of paying them a visit at Lauieville, and had a pleasant meeting again with old friends, particularly the cyclists and signallers again. They too had been in the thick of the fighting on the Somme, but were then resting, being bivouacked among the corn 'stooks' of a harvest field. The 1st Camerons, having been rested, and strengthened by more drafts, were soon making preparations for another turn up the line. It was now the beginning of September and the weather had been very wet, leaving the roads in a bad state, when we left Albert and marched to Behencourt. We stayed here a few days without doing any fighting, and then moved back to Millincourt, the rumour being that we were going back for a six week's rest.

The signal section was billeted in a barn, and we had a few easy days until we got marching orders in a hurry, and at 4am one morning we were roused by the full band playing 'Reveille'. By 5am we were packed up and on the road, marching to Bresle where we went into billets. At Bresle gangs of German prisoners were at work cleaning and repairing the roads under the charge of French sentries, who saw there was no slackness in their work. On the day following our arrival, we had Church Service in a field and orders for moving again came in.

19

On the Somme

Leaving Bresle in the afternoon, we marched in heavy rain, and over almost impassible roads to Becourt Wood. We expected to get billets in some old wooden shelters, but there were not enough to go round, and the signallers were lucky to find room in an old cook-house in a trench called 'Tiger Pop'. What with being wet to the skin, and everything around us in a soaking condition, we were in a very miserable state but we set to work and built a great roaring fire to dry and warm ourselves, while the rain kept pouring down all night. We rested the next day in preparation for entering the front line at night. At 7 o'clock in the evening we set off to relieve the Norfolks whose position was supposed to be somewhere in front of High Wood. Owing to the heavy fighting in the sector at this time, the front line was never long in the same place. Old trenches were constantly being blown up by shell fire, and new ones dug every night, so that it was no light task finding the men we were to relieve. The whole valley of the Somme at this time was little better than a sea of mud, and roads were terrible to march over. Passing through 'Death Valley', strewn with the dead bodies of men and horses, and the wreckage of transport columns, with now and then great bursting shells falling around us, we struggled as best we could till dark. To try and keep as dry as possible we walked along the edge of the trenches feeling our way cautiously forward in the darkness. All went well until we got quite close to High Wood, when some shells landed a few score yards to our right. At this, the officer in charge ordered us into the communication trench for safety. For a few minutes, we scrambled along through mud and water up to our waists. After such a hard march, it was now midnight, this almost finished us, and we cursed the officer for having ordered us into such a place. At last, completely exhausted, we reached the wood which had previously been a German strong-hold. The wood was now reduced to a tangled mass of broken trees, and smashed wire defences, through which, in various directions, ran lines of trenches. Guides were to meet us, and lead us to the front lines, but we could find none of these, so we set off to locate the Norfolks ourselves.

Never, so long as they live, will any of 'A' Coy, to which Monteith and I had been attached as signallers, forget the horrors of that night. We were round the wood and through the wood, over and over again, but never a Norfolk man could we find. We tripped and fell over barbed wire, into trenches, over tree stumps, rose and tripped again the whole night through. The trenches were full of bodies both British and German. They lay in grotesque shapes, some indeed stood propped against the parapet, and more than once in the inky darkness we spoke to men who were beyond the power of answering our questions. Always there was the possibility of us running into the enemy lines, we were all strangers to the ground, so we tried to make as little noise as possible. Added to the invisible uncertainties, and terrors of the night, arose the nauseating stink of the dead and rotting human flesh. Small wonder men's hair turned grey in a night.

As dawn was beginning to show in the east, Capt Elliott with his company took possession of an old trench, and Monteith and I were told to make our way back to Hqrs. We had been struggling along from 7pm till 5am and were glad to see the welcome daylight. The pair of us made ourselves comfortable in an old dug-out to the west of 'High Wood', set about making some tea, and after a good meal we lay down and slept quite soundly, all unconcerned about the shells that screeched and whined around us. After a few days of 'holding on' to this position, during which the regiment was heavily shelled almost incessantly, and received a heavy casualty list, we heard that the 1st Glosters would relieve us, for which we were not sorry. A few yards from the dug-out, in which Jimmy and I had taken up our quarters, was a monster shell hole into which 14 of the biggest men I ever saw had been dragged. They were all members of the Kaiser's famous 'Prussian Guards', killed in the first battle for 'High Wood'. This was only one of the awful sights in the vicinity. Wandering round one day I saw a pair of officer's riding boots and, thinking they might be of some use, I stooped to pick them up, only to find they contained a man's leg shot off by the knee. It was at 'High Wood', properly called Foreau Wood, where I first saw tanks in action and two of them got stranded in the middle of the tree stumps and trenches. The ammunition in these was set on fire by German artillery fire, and for a long time we could hear the 'pop', 'pop' of the cartridges as the heat reached and exploded them. At midnight on September 21st, the 'Glosters' relieved us, and the Camerons moved back about a mile to a sunken road known as Chester Street. Jimmy and I stayed all night in our own dug-out before going back to the battalion. Next day the 1st Brigade Hqrs, located in an old shell-shattered house at Bazentin-le-Grande was destroyed by enemy shells, and as we rested we watched and criticised the marksmanship of his artillery. From Chester Street, we had a good view of a large portion of the Somme battlefield, such famous places as Longueval, Delville Wood, Courcelette, all lying within view, with the woods of Bazentin behind, and the wreckage of High Wood in front of us. Villages and woods had been levelled almost to the ground, only a few bricks showing where peaceful country homes once stood, and tree stumps with here an isolated tree, and there a cluster of undergrowth, mutely marking the place where lovely woods had flourished. A more bleak and desolated spot could not be imagined, and certainly not described in words. In the wood of Bazentin we found artificial trees of steel, which had been erected and used by the Germans as observation posts. I also came across a Britisher and a German who had fought hand to hand, each dying with his bayonet driven through the body of his adversary. Truly two brave men they must have been.

Each night, while out of the actual firing line, we had to supply 'working parties', either for trench digging, or to assist the engineers in dug-out or defensive construction. We always reckoned it was safer in the firing line than going out with a working party, as these often got into exposed positions, and once noticed by the enemy, stood a poor chance of regaining safety without loss. While at Chester Street, we lost 24 men killed in one night on a working party, and the same night two men were killed in their sleep, so there was no safety wherever we were. The 24th saw us relieved by the 1st Northamptons, and we went further back to 'Mametz Wood'. A rest here for two days, and we had orders to stand by in support of the 2nd Brigade in expectation of a German attack, but this came to nothing, and on the 27th we left Mametz and marched back through Fricourt and Albert to Bresle. This demanded a long and trying journey, burdened as we were with full packs and equipment. At Bresle our billets were condemned, and two companies moved out to tents in Bresle Woods, while the remainder followed next day. The continuous inclement weather at this time made camp life anything but pleasant for us. Sunday morning was notable for our first Church Parade for some weeks, while in the afternoon we played the Black Watch at football. Next morning, we signallers were ordered to parade before the 'C.O.', and there was much speculation as to what 'we were up for'. After the usual inspection, Col. Craig-Brown said why we had been paraded was to allow him to thank us, as a section, for the good work we had done during the hard fighting of the past few weeks. This was praise we hadn't expected, though it is true we had done 'our bit', like all others of the regiment.

20
A month's rest

On Monday, October 2nd, our transport left for Abbeville, in preparation for the division going out for a rest of which we all stood in need, and our spirits rose high at the thought of leaving the Somme battlefield for a time. On the 3rd we made an early start, reveille going at 4am and by 6 o'clock we had breakfasted, got all packed up, and were really on our way for divisional rest. On the Albert–Amiens road, we mounted a fleet of motor-buses about 10 o'clock. These buses were originally omnibuses were originally plying the streets of London, and it was something new for us to be carried to our destination, instead of marching. The trip by bus produced some comical incidents. Being heavily laden, one or other of them often stuck by the way, while the others kept going ahead, the men cheering their more unfortunate companions for the time being. On the way, we passed gangs of prisoners engaged in road repairs, and shepherded by French soldiers. An unusual thing that took our eye was the row of fruit trees, generally apple trees, which bordered either side of the long straight road, while growing behind these again, were the tall poplars for which France is famous. We passed by many small villages, and through the towns of Amiens and Abbeville before reaching Saigneville.

Saigneville is a village situated a short distance from the mouth of the River Somme, a quiet country spot far removed from the battle-front. It was 6 o'clock in the evening and getting dusk when we arrived after a long journey which left us cramped and stiff. The battalion was billeted in various buildings in the village, and we signallers found quarters in a barn at a small farm. The following day was an easy one for us, spent chiefly in making ourselves acquainted with the village and its surroundings. How different it all seemed to the villages in the war zone. In this old-fashioned out-of-the-way hamlet everything and everyone was at peace. The slow easy-going folks were busily engaged in gathering their harvest of apples, which we learned were carted away to be made into cider. The people took kindly to us and we mixed with them freely, and made many new friends. From now onwards during our rest, we had a daily routine of parades to go through. With the signal section, I had a fairly easy time. In Lt McInnes we had a good officer who did not trouble us much, so long as we were proficient in our work. Much of our inside work was done in the village 'estaminet' or inn, where we had the warmth of a good stove, but most of all, I think we enjoyed our station work in the open fields, for which we used flags, lamps and heliographs. One day we marched via Cahon and Lambercourt to a brewery at Miannay, where we enjoyed a refreshing bath. Near the village was an aerodrome and I remember as we marched along the road having to scatter for safety, as an aeroplane in attempting to land, crossed the road and ran through our ranks. On the 14th October, 'D' Coy held some sports at which I won the half-mile, and was second in the quarter-mile race. Being a stranger in the company I created a good deal of surprise by beating the man who for years had been the recognised champion half-miler of the 1st Camerons. The sports ground was a stubble field, and part of the track was ploughed land, so it was no easy race. The signal officer, himself a 'D' Coy man, was very pleased at my success, and in offering his congratulations remarked that 'he'd just like to have the "wind" that I had'.

About this time a 'dry canteen' was set up by the officers for the benefit of the men, and Monteith, who was a grocer, was put in charge of it. In his absence from the section I made great friends with Jimmy Sharp, and he and I had some fine times together. Nothing suited us better than to go off walking, and visit the different villages round about. Two favourites were Mons Bourbour and Quesnoy, and we often tramped out to these when our work for the day was over. On the 21st the battalion was Inspected by the Divisional Commander, Maj. Gen Strickland and after the inspection two Military Crosses and six Military Medals were presented to officers and men respectively, for bravery at 'High Wood' on September 3rd. Two of the latter were signallers named Williams and Hosie. On Sunday, Church Parade being cancelled on account of a heavy shower of rain, Monteith, Sharp and myself went off walking along the Somme Canal to St Valery, a small port at the mouth of the River Somme, and here we spent a very enjoyable afternoon. The sight of the sea made us wish perhaps, that we could cross right over the Channel to the land right opposite, that meant so much to each of us, but when we had tired of looking seawards there was nothing left for us but to return to billets. We were now nearing the end of October and our rest was getting pretty well through. This meant that we should soon be back in action, and the regiment, having been reinforced to normal strength by drafts, was now in spick and span condition and full of fight. The change had done us all good, and there was a freshness and briskness about the battalion which contrasted favourably with the tired and battered regiment that went to Saigneville. Away from the battle line, the memories of the awful sights we had seen and lived through, had been softened by our month of quietness, and we were now as new men. Parting gifts from the villagers were showered upon us as we made preparations for departure, and one thing always sends my mind back to Saigneville, and that is an apple; for there we ate many a stone of good ripe fruit, and carried as many as possible away with us.

21

More of the Somme

We left Saigneville on the last day of October, and again we journeyed by bus, travelling by way of Airanes and Amiens to our old halting place at Bresle. Leaving the buses here, we marched to Henincourt Wood and were billeted in wooden huts. The whole camp was in a very bad state, being little better than a mud-hole. The day following our arrival was a holiday, and in the evening Sharp and I, on the prowl as usual, went to the village of Warloy, and noticing the Church lit up, we entered and found ourselves in the midst of a Catholic service, but no one took exception to us as we joined the congregation.

For a few days, we had the usual parades and here our signal sergeant received his commission, but though the promotion took him from amongst us to the signal section, he still remained the same old 'Pip' Pollok. On Sunday, November 5th, we left Henincourt Wood and relieved the 15th Division in Becourt Wood, where we went into tents. The weather was very bad, each day being wetter than another, and it was extremely uncomfortable living in tents, especially when 14 men with all their kit were crowded into one tent. The battalion was put on fatigue duty, salvage work, and road making at Becourt, and at Contalmaison. On the 9th we moved into newly built huts at Becourt Camp and these were much more comfortable than tents, as they were fitted up with stoves. There was a combined church service on Sunday 12th for the whole brigade, music being supplied by the brass band of the Black Watch.

The signal section spent much time salvaging telephone wire of which there were miles and miles, lying on the ground in all directions, but this was much easier work than making roads with the rest of the battalion. The regiment went into action again on the 17th Nov, taking over the front line in front of the 'Butte-de-Warlencourt', with the famous High Wood away on our right. The

'Butte' was a solitary hill held by the Germans, and it was a real stronghold. Various attempts had been made to capture it, but so far it had proved too strong. From it the enemy looked down into our lines, and they were able to throw 'pine-apple' bombs right amongst us as they pleased, so we were in a very hot corner. I was attached to 'B' Coy as signaller in the front line, and it became so dangerous there that we moved a little distance back into Abbey Trench, but before the night was over the whole trench was blown to pieces, and we suffered many losses in killed and wounded. As usual I was one of the lucky ones, and escaped unhurt, saving also my telephone from the wreckage. The captain of 'B' Coy sent me back to Hqrs after this, and I remember sleeping on the stairway of a deep dug-out for a few hours. Early in the morning I was sent in charge of 3 men to carry hot tea and rum to the front line. The trenches of the Somme battlefield were in a fearful state, owing to the prevailing wet weather, and the communication trench used by us and named Pioneer Alley was worse than most of them. So bad was it at this stage, that I decided to lead my little expedition over the top, so that we might travel with all possible speed. Our journey to the front was safe and uneventful as we followed the route of communication trench and after delivering the tea and rum, we turned about to go back. We were hurrying to reach Hqrs before daylight, when our attention was drawn to two men in a trench we were passing. On examination we found they were both stuck hard and fast in the mud in which they had been standing up to their waists for some hours. They were members of a party who had been relieved about midnight, and now, they had given up hopes of being rescued alive. Their strength was done, and our efforts to haul them out were of no use, until we leaned over the edge of the trench and unbuckled their equipments, and loosened the great-coats they wore. After that, our united efforts managed to drag them free, but we left the coats and equipment sticking in the mire. Giving them directions how to reach Hqrs, we hurried on as fast as possible. Dawn was now breaking, and to be seen on the top was like asking to be shot. Just a little further on we found two more fast in the mud, and to these also we gave a helping hand, though their plight was not near so bad as the first pair. I was indeed glad when our exciting trip was ended, and we had safely regained Headquarters ourselves, which later that day moved back to dug-outs in Starfish Trench.

22

Rough times in the trenches

Life in the trenches at this time was very hard, and very disheart-ening, while the weather was of the most disagreeable order. We were continually under enemy fire, not the rifle fire of a year before, but the devastating fire of all manner of artillery. Day by day, we lost men killed and wounded, and we never knew who would be knocked out next. In Starfish Trench the accommoda-tion for men was very limited, and I remember sharing, with three others, a shallow hole like a cupboard cut in the side of the trench, in which, we half-sat, half-laid, when supposed to be sleeping, with our legs hanging down the side of the trench, so that most of the time we were wet through. The slightest concussion from a shell dropping near would have destroyed our humble shelter, but luckily we escaped that catastrophe. At night the 'star shells' or 'very' lights seemed to burst above us, so near were we to the enemy lines. Truly it was an eerie place. Close by was a large dump of war material, bombs, grenades and small arms ammunition by the thousand rounds, also immense quantities of barbed wire and angle iron used in the construction of front line defences. Here, too, were capacious tanks, always full of fresh water for the use of the various battalions in the front line. At night the 'Nine Elms' dump, so called from the straggling row of elm trees growing near, was a scene of great activity, as parties coming from the front trenches made the dump a rendezvous, where they met their transport limbers, and, having collected their rations and stores, departed again with as little noise as possible. Often enough, the enemy who probably knew exactly what was going on, sent over a few shells, and many a poor fellow was laid low while on a 'ration party'. After spending a few wretched days in Starfish trench, we left in small parties early one morning, and proceeded to Mametz Wood, where we were billeted in tents. This spell in tents was easily the worst I ever experienced. For a week or two we never knew what it was to be dry and comfortable. The old tents were useless against an unceasing downpour of rain. Many men were down with sickness, due to the exposure we had to face. Night after night, we paraded with shovels and marched up to the trenches, where we tried to clear the mud from the trench bottoms. We might as well have worked amongst putty, as we could hardly get the shovels either in or out of the sticky mud. Our feet and legs were often held fast as well, and it was really a most heart-breaking task. None of us were at all sorry when orders came for us to leave Mametz Wood, even though the next move was forward towards the firing line.

On November 27th, I was one of a billeting party which took over newly built huts near High Wood, where we relieved the men of the 1st South Wales Borderers, belonging to the 3rd Brigade. Next day, came one of those little adventures in which I escaped death by the proverbial hair's-breadth. I was detailed in the after-noon as one of a working party for the Engineers in front of Longueval. We left camp at 3.30 in the afternoon, and after a long tramp through muddy communication trenches, we were met by an engineer officer, who took charge and directed us in the work to be done. This consisted of carrying heavy timber to the front line, for the making of deep dug-outs, for by this time we had begun to copy the German idea of building deep and safe shelters for the men in the firing line. It was now dark, and slowly in single file, we made our way forward with many a trip, and many a fall. Light shells whizzed past us at intervals in the darkness, but we knew they were random shots so far as we were concerned, and we plodded along. Our second and final journey was finished about 8pm, and we were feeling thankful that our day's work was done. On our way back, we had occasion to cross one of those innumerable 'sunken roads' so often met with in France. The earthy sides of this road were soft and slippery, and the engineer officer was very kindly helping each man to clamber up with the aid of his stick. It happened I was the last man of the party, and as I caught hold of his stick to haul myself up the bank, a shell plunged into the earth just beneath my foot. For a fraction of time I waited, as did the officer, for the bursting of the shell, till it dawned on us that it was a 'dud', and our lives were spared in consequence. 'Thank Heaven for "dud" shells' said the officer. Had the shell burst, although only of a light variety, it was quite heavy enough to blow the pair of us to pieces. Apparently my luck, which our signallers swore by, still held good. This was not our only adventure that night, as on the return journey, the party got lost in some old trenches, and it was well into morning when we finally reached camp. We remained on fatigue duties for some days, till, on December 1st we were shelled out of our huts on two occasions. A comical incident occurred when the Sgt Major's tent was hoisted on to a telephone wire by a shell, where it hung fluttering in the breeze. That night we relieved the 1st Gloucesters in front of the Butte-de-Warlencourt. For one night I stayed at Hqrs and went out to Switch Dump with a party of men to draw rations. On the night of Sunday 3rd, I went, in company with Bill Sawdon, to relieve Monteith and Percy Carruthers at a signal station in the front line. The wires to this particular station were 'dis' – the signallers word for disconnected, and to spare the linesmen going out, I agreed to go over the top to the front line and examine the wire. Bill accompanied me with some misgivings. He was a married man, which may have accounted for his nervousness, especially at night, while I had the name of a 'devil-may-care'. Certainly the danger in anything never worried me. However, off we went, loaded up with our equipment, our rifles, and each carrying a bag of rations, together with various signalling stores. The night was very dark except for the occasional glimmer of a 'star-shell'. On our right we could hear the low voices of men as the companies relieved each other by way of 'Pioneer Alley', while now and then great shells crashed and burst quite near to us. Running the wire through my hand we made our way forward till we came to the break caused by a bursting shell, which had thrown the broken ends far apart. Groping round in the darkness I failed to find the other end of the wire. Bill began to get impatient, and urged me to leave it, but that would have been madness, and to sit in the front line with-out any communications to Hqrs, might have meant the loss of a company or more, should 'Jerry' make an attack. For a long time I searched in a widening circle for the missing end, until Bill, holding the other, began to cry like a child, and threatened to leave me. I told him if he let go of the wire I'd shoot and that steadied him a little. Eventually, I found the loose end of the wire, and soon had a connection made. We then hurried forward, and in due course arrived at the 'station'. Entering we asked if they were 'through', but they said 'No'. However, on testing, we found to our relief, the line was then alright. Poor old Bill Sawdon was glad to get into shelter, but often in later times when speaking of the adventure, he said 'Nothing on earth would persuade him to go with me on a night expedition among telephone lines again'. Perhaps I was rather hard on him that night. During the night our wires were smashed again, and just as dawn was breaking I went over the top, and taking the line in my hand, I made my way as quickly as possible in the direction of Hqrs, with the intention of repairing the damage. The wires lay only a short distance from the communication trench, and who should I see there in the grey of the morning, but our C.O. going the round of the trenches. He pulled me up, and asked why I was running about without 'arms'. I explained that the telephone wires were broken and I was depending on speed to do the necessary repairs, and to carry a rifle and ammunition would be a hindrance rather than any help. The 'C.O.' smiled. 'You know the risk you run?' he said. 'Yes sir.' 'Well be careful; good morning'. Many an officer would have had me put under arrest, for being without my rifle, but Col

Craig-Brown, as an old signaller himself, knew our difficulties. I soon had the wire put in order and got safely back to the front line, where for two days Sawdon and I kept up good communications with Hqrs, and on the third night after being heavily bombed from the 'Butte', the company we were attached to, 'B' Coy, were relieved by 'A' Coy, and we moved back to the support lines at 'Flers Line'. I remember as Bill and I went down the duckboard track that frosty morning, and with snow lying thick on the ground, I stepped off the track at a right-angle turn of the boards into a shell-hole full of icy-cold water, which soaked me to the hips. When I got scrambled out again, I was a bedraggled specimen of a Highlander as I trudged uncomfortably on in my wet kilt. After calling at Hqrs, for our rations, we found a decent shelter with the officers' cooks, and had a royal time for a day or two. In Flers Line, it was rather quieter than the trenches close to the Butte de Warlencourt, but after a couple of days, we were relieved by the Black Watch, and went round by High Wood, to some huts at Bazentin-le-Petit. Here, we experienced more wild weather, while we were kept busy digging drains, laying duckboard tracks, and carrying firewood to the cookers. All this sort of work while we were supposed to be resting; truly there was no peace on the Somme battlefield. Christmas Day found us due to go back to the fighting line. There was no Xmas fare for us that time, none of the good things to be had, usually associated with that festive season. In the evening, we relieved the Glosters in Flers Switch, in which we were very heavily shelled, and suffered severe losses. On the 28th our 'B' Coy relieved a company of the 8th Berkshires in Flers Line, while 'D' Coy went into reserve in Eaucourt l'Abbaye, an old mansion which had been levelled to the ground, and of which, only the cellars remained, but these formed a safe shelter, being practically shell proof. During this spell I had for partner a Yorkshire lad named Plackett. The trenches were waist deep in mud and conditions generally were terrible. Looking back on those days it seems marvellous how men kept going at all. On December 30th the 1st Div. was relieved by the 50th and the 7th Northumberland

Fusiliers relieved the Camerons. It so happened that no signallers came to relieve Plackett and myself when the company was relieved, and we had to wait until the new men were settled and then ask for relief over the 'phone. It was midnight when the pair of us set off for the huts at Bazentin; the last two of the Camerons to leave the Somme. We buoyed ourselves up with the thought that we'd be able to call at a soup kitchen on our way, for we were both tired and hungry, but after going off the track for half-a-mile we found the soup kitchen closed and deserted. After a few minutes rest, we gathered up our traps and staggered along in the dark to Bazentin. Next day, the last of the old year, the whole battalion marched via Becordel, and Fricourt, to Albert, and took billets in old ruined houses, almost roofless perhaps, but still better than the cold trenches. What did we care, though we had nothing to sleep on but stone floors, we'd slept in worse places up the Somme, and it was a relief to get our clothes off – the first time for weeks. Far into the night we laughed and joked, alternately telling each other of adventures that had befallen us. We had foraged round for wood, and roaring fires were kept going, while we felt as happy, for the time being, as schoolboys on holiday. Only at times was there a touch of sadness, as we recalled lost comrades, for we had buried more than the strength of the regiment on those terrible valleys and ridges. All our work had consisted of holding ground others had taken, and I can safely say, we never let go a yard of it.

23

Moving around

In passing, I might mention that a large wooden monument in the shape of St Andrews Cross was erected to the memory of the Cameron Highlanders, who fell in defence of ground at High Wood. This bore a Gaelic inscription meaning 'To the brave who are no more'. The monument was destroyed later during the German offensive in 1917. A photo of the cross is my memento of hard fighting at High Wood.

We spent New Years Day 1917 resting after our long hard spell in the fighting line, and took the chance of cleaning ourselves and our clothes as well as we could. There were no festivities, as there had been no opportunities for preparing them. It was sufficient for us, to be out of the trenches. Next day, the battalion paraded, company by company, for baths. In the evening Jimmy Sharp and I went to the Divnl Cinema, and both enjoyed our visit to the 'pictures'.

For a day or two, we were busily engaged in refitting. Most of our clothes were in rags and large quantities of uniforms were necessary to remedy our defects, and deficiencies in clothing. On January 3rd, I visited a large salvage dump for the purpose of exchanging some damaged equipment, and found, to my surprise and pleasure, that the N.C.O., in charge was an old school-mate, John Emmerson, then a Cpl in the Northumberland Fusiliers. As natives of the same parish, we found much in common to speak of, and his was the first Cumbrian face I had seen in France for many a day. For some few days, we did only light parades, the battalion was in a sort of convalescent stage, but gradually recovering from battle-weariness. Sometimes, the R.S.M. would take us on parade and put us through our paces, but it was always a pleasure to work to his commands. Most of my time, however was spent in signalling work. Communication was of course always maintained with the different battalions in the vicinity, whether in the fighting line or out of it, and besides, we had to keep up our efficiency in field work, always providing for the day when trench fighting would cease, and we should return to open warfare. On the 10th, we left Albert and took the place of the Black Watch in the huts at Fricourt. We were now experiencing severe winter weather, and there were heavy falls of snow and rain. This confined our signalling activities to indoor work with telephones, while our leisure in the evenings was generally spent in the Y.M.C.A. Hut, where we often had concerts and 'sing-songs'. On the 14th, I visited my old pals of the 6th Battalion, who lay close by at Scots Redoubt. Days of indoor work followed except for the odd times when we were out on fatigue duty. The weather got steadily colder, and frost and snow continued, so we were glad to be out of the trenches for the time being. On the 24th, we were witnesses of an exciting scene in connection with our observation balloons. Owing to the pressure of the very high winds, one of the mooring chains broke, and a balloon began to rise rapidly among the clouds. The two balloonists made desperate efforts to bring their balloon to earth by allowing gas to escape, but the wind was too strong, and the 'gas bag' began to turn over and over, as it soared skywards. At last, one man jumped out in a parachute, and landed safely about a mile on our right. His companion by some means lost his parachute, and we watched the balloon with the second man still aboard, being blown like a feather away towards the Channel. Its fate, and that of the unfortunate balloonist, could only be surmised. Next day, we were relieved by men of the 1st Australian Division. Fricourt was left behind at 8.30 in the morning, and we marched via Albert, and along the Amiens road through the village of Lauieville to Warloy. It was a bitterly cold day, but the roads being frozen hard were good to march along. Our billets at Warloy were cold, draughty, outbuildings belonging to farms, and there were no fires allowed. So severe was the frost that even our bread was as hard as stones after lying in the billet all night. One afternoon, the signallers walked out to an aerodrome and played a football match against men of the Flying Corps, beating them by 3 goals to 1.

For the week commencing January 29th, I took over Battalion Orderly Cpl from Jimmy Monteith, so for one week I was clear of parades, but instead, had to take charge of the 'sick parade', draw the rations for the battalion, also the mails, and deliver the day's orders to all companies. On the 31st I played football for the signal section against the Glosters whom we beat 4–1. In the evening, I was sent to take charge of the company messengers or 'runners', as we called them, who were not turning out very well in the mornings for their work. The billet they occupied was worse, if anything, than the one I had left, and at night the rats ran over us in swarms so there was not much rest, or sleep, for us. Outside the snow was lying thickly, and it remained bitterly cold. Parades of the ordinary kind were almost useless, our hands being too numb to permit of handling rifles, so we went in more for sports to keep ourselves warm. Cross-country running, and football, with occasional route marches helped to keep us from being starved, and also kept us in hard and fit condition.

During our stay here our C.O. left to take command of a brigade in Salonika, taking with him the good wishes of all the battalion. Soon after this, we were glad to have orders to leave Warloy, and on Sunday 4th of February, we packed up once more, and began to move forward, passing through Ribemont, Mericourt, Sailly-le-See, to a camp near Cerisy, 15 kilometres distant. After a halt of two days, during which we had the usual parades and an inspection by a French General, we left this camp, and marched via Cerisy, Morcourt, Mericourt-sur-Somme and Chuignolles to Marly Camp, and were billeted in large French huts. These were much too large and airy to be comfortable during winter weather, so next day we moved into billets in the village of Chuignolles. During the night, we had a visit from German bombing 'planes, but although many bombs were dropped in the vicinity, we suffered no casualties. For some days, we had a quiet uneventful time doing various drills, while great attention was paid to the handling and rapid fixing on of gas masks, for at this time gas was being used with deadly effect by both armies. At the neighbouring village of Chuignes, stood the divisional baths, and here we enjoyed a glorious hot bath, and received special treatment for the feet. On the 13th the regiment had a field day in conjunction with the rest of the brigade and during these mimic operations we were bombed in reality by enemy aeroplanes. The same night orders came to enter the fighting line in a new sector.

24

On the Assevilliers Front

The 24th of February found us marching into action again. We passed through the ruined villages of Dompierre, and Assevilliers, round which were many belts of barbed wire defences. Near an old sugar refinery, which showed the marks of much battering by guns, we found the lonely grave of a 2nd Cameron, and some of our 'Old Contemptibles' could remember the 2nd Battalion, then in Salonika, being in this district during the early days of the war. Previous to the 1st Division taking over this sector, it had been held by French Troops, and the trenches bore some strange names. The first we entered was called 'Boyau Martinique' and here we relieved the 1st Northamptons, and were in support of the Black Watch. The fighting line was fairly quiet here, so quiet that it seemed like a calm before a storm.

Jimmy Sharp and I were attached to 'B' Coy as signallers, and on the third night of our stay here, a shell landed on the top of our dug-out, but luckily we were too deep down below the surface for any damage being done. On the 18th, the Germans spotted one of our working parties, and promptly shelling it, caused 6 casualties. In the evening, we relieved the Black Watch in the front line, going forward by way Boyau Reunion, and Noumea trenches. The frosty weather had now gone, and, in the thaw and rain which followed, the trenches began to cave in at the sides, and consequently became very muddy. Each day they seemed to get worse, and notes in my diary describe them as 'like a swimming bath'. I remember one day there was to be a 'test' gas message, the object of which was to find out how quickly the message could be sent round, and every man be wearing his mask. We signallers knew it was only for practice, and were prepared for it. Our instructions were to hand it to the first person we saw, after receiving it by 'phone. Sharp, who was on duty at the time, read off the message, and I dashed outside with it, and handed it to a passing officer, saying as I did so – 'Gas!' The officer made as if to run off at full speed, but unluckily for him, he caught his foot in the woodwork at the side of the trench, and went sprawling his length in a great pool of mud and water. This caused a little delay to the message, but Sharp and I had a good laugh at the officer, as he got up and shook himself like a dog. After some very miserable days the Black Watch came in and relieved us, and the Camerons went out to dug-outs in Assevilliers. Everybody was in a very wet and dirty state, as often on our way out of the communi-cation trenches we were wading waist deep in mud and water. There were many almost at their last gasp before they got out that night, while one man in particular had discarded his equipment, and also his uniform, in order to walk more freely, and all he possessed on coming out was his gas helmet, his shirt and his boots. The transport officer, and some of his men, came to act as guides to the dug outs, and they carried the weakest men on their backs. Throughout the following few days, we had the usual fatigue work to perform, but we signallers escaped much of this by doing salvage work among telephone wire. Wire was a very necessary part of our stores, and we took every opportunity of reeling up as much of the best of it, as we could find. On the 27th of February we went into the trenches again, taking over our old position from the Black Watch. Once more, Sharp and I were attached to 'B' Coy, in support to the rest of the battalion and located in 'Gorizia' trench. Things were again surprisingly quiet, though a German aeroplane caused some excitement one day by dashing over and bringing to earth one of our observation balloons. It was a daring piece of work, and in spite of all the anti-aircraft guns that were turned upon him, the airman made good his escape. On the 2nd of March I was a witness of a piece of good work by our artillery, acting under directions given by one of our scouts. This scout, who was on duty in an observation post near our dug out, at dawn 'spotted' an enemy working party making their way to-wards the trenches. Immediately ringing up Hqrs I explained the position, and gave the map reference, while they passed on the information to the artillery. Picking up my glasses I then ran out to the observation post to watch results. Slowly and unthinkingly the German party walked along the road distant about 3 miles from us, when suddenly 'Bang! Bang! Bang! Bang!', one round battery fire was fired at them. When the smoke lifted, only a few 'Jerries' were to be seen running for their lives, but most of them had been knocked out by the splendid shooting of our gunners. The 1st Brigade was relieved on March 4th, and the 2nd Munster Fusiliers took over from us in the front line while we went back to Assevilliers for the night. Next day the 2nd Welsh Regt took our places, and we marched back to Chuignes, and were billeted in huts. We were now clear of the trenches, our brigade being in divisional reserve, and so we found ourselves in training in readiness for an attack on the Assevilliers front. This was what we had been expecting for some time, as it was suspected the enemy was up to some mischief or other, on this sector. Our signalling preparations, which included much visual work gave us the idea there would be a big advance. On the 10th, the battalion marched in companies to Dompierre, where we were fitted out with new box respirators. During the next week I was Hqr Orderly Sgt, and so escaped the ordinary routine. On Sunday 11th, we had Church Service in the morning in the lines of the 10th Glosters, and had a bathing parade at Chuignes in the afternoon. On the 12th, we relieved the Kings Royal Rifles at Dompierre, and here we were in reserve to the remainder of the 1st Brigade, while for a day or two we had peace and quietness. My duties as orderly sergeant here, were very trying. It was anything but pleasant, to hunt for the various sections in the darkness for the purpose of delivering orders for the following day. I was continually falling into holes and old trenches, and it was generally midnight when I got finished with my duties. We relieved the Black Watch in the front line on the night of the 15th, Sharp and I again going in with 'B' Coy. Although we had not actually been told, we had an idea there would be some excitement for us this spell. The Black Watch had reported everything very quiet, and so we were all on edge to know what was going to happen. On the night of the 16th March I received instructions from the Signal

Officer to proceed to a certain point in the front line, and be prepared for anything. It seemed a strange order, but with the good wishes of Sharp I set off at 4am, wondering what was to happen, and where the adventure would lead me. Arriving at the appointed place, where I had expected to find another signaller, I found all quiet and not a man to be found anywhere. This puzzled me, but on hunting around, I came across a newly laid telephone wire, which pointed to some of our fellows being near at hand somewhere. The light was now breaking so I set off to find where the new line led to. After going some distance along the trench, I was amazed to find the line go up and over the top. This, together with the fact that all was still, and I had, as yet, encountered not a single man, gave me much to think about, but I reasoned that if the man who laid the wire could go over the top, then so could I, and over I went. Another surprise awaited me as not a shot was fired at me crossing 'no man's land'. Following the course of the telephone wire I duly arrived at the German front line, realising by this time, although I had still seen no one, that there had been an advance during the night. From the first line trench into the second line, and then further back to the third line, I cautiously followed the wire, and at the end of it found Kinghorn – one of our signallers – sitting quite composed with his 'phone in a 'Jerry' dug-out and wondering what was to be done next. Very briefly he gave me the news 'D' Coy had been detailed to raid the enemy lines at 2am for the purpose of finding out what the enemy was up to and, if possible, capture some prisoners. Their attempt had been met with terrible machine-gun fire, and they had been driven back, but trying again at 4am, they were able to cross over without a shot being fired. The enemy had retired quickly and completely behind the line of the Somme Canal, leaving us nothing but empty trenches. It had been a cunning move and well executed. Leaving Kinghorn, I hurried back to our own lines with the news. The captain of 'B' Coy was amazed when I said I had been to the enemy third line trenches. 'Are you sure?' he asked, when I had told him about my trip across 'no man's land'. 'Quite sure Sir' I answered, while at the same time I handed over a German paper and some postcards I had taken from an undistributed bag of mails in the enemy trenches. In a few minutes, he had gathered together the company bombers, and I went as guide for the party I had hard work to persuade the Captain that it was safe to cross the ground between ours and the German lines, such a thing in the ordinary course in daylight would have been suicidal for any who attempted it, but in the end he took my word for it, and we went across to where 'D' Coy had taken possession of the enemy position. Except for occasional shells from long-range guns, which did no harm, the day passed over very quietly, while we advanced steadily, yet with caution, always on the look-out for a trap. The village of Barleux was entered without opposition and beyond it we came to the most perfect barbed-wire defensive system I had yet seen. It stretched to the right and left as far as the eye could see, and varied in depth from 30 to 40 yards. Composed of the roughest and most destructive wire imaginable, it would have proved a very serious obstacle to pass in a fight. Cunningly contrived openings had been made through it here and there in zig-zag fashion. These apertures had of course been made for the benefit of patrols, but at first glance these were indistinguishable, even in daylight. Towards evening, we were out in open country, and halted for the night in some old trenches. Rations arrived, and were served out and for once and with good reason everybody was in great spirits. Seldom had we advanced so swiftly and so far without casualties, and being rather excited at this strange turn of events, wondered how far we should go before getting in touch with 'our friends the enemy'. In the darkness of night we could see the glare in the sky from great fires as the Germans burned the villages while retreating. The next day we found the brigades on each side of us had advanced to such a position, that we had practically been cut out of the line, and on being relieved by the 8th Royal Berkshire Regiment, we moved back to the old British lines. While the advance still continued, the 1st Division slipped quietly into corps reserve. Cavalry and artillery were now pushing forward in large numbers to the banks of the

Somme Canal. On March 21st we relieved the 6th Welsh Fusiliers, and for some days were very busy with railway construction work at Fay and also at Dompierre. The weather, being extremely cold, made this work very dull and monotonous. On the 26th, I found myself in isolation owing to an outbreak of measles among the officers. This was something out of the common, but not being affected myself was content to wait and see what happened. The 29th of March found the battalion on the move again, and with the 'isolation party' at a safe distance in the rear, we marched from Dompierre via Foucaucourt, along the St Quentin–Amiens road through Framerville and Vauvillers to Rosieres. I found myself in a good billet, as billets went in France, in what had once been a stylish house, but was now badly smashed, as were most other buildings of this little town. We were now on the old battlefields of 1914, and here the French and Germans had fought some bitter engagements. On the 31st, along with 6 officers' servants, cook, and mess waiter, I was taken by ambulance car to the 2nd Field Amb. at Marly Camp, and the whole lot were placed in quarantine, in a large marquee. For a week, we had an exceedingly quiet time, having little to do but read and write, while outside the weather was very severe, rain, hail and snow falling heavily. On April 9th we returned to our battalion by motor car, the route taking us through Proyart, Framerville, and Rosieres, to Rouy-le-Petit, to which village the battalion had moved during our absence.

25

Work and play

At Rouy-le-Petit the Camerons seemed to be lying spare, and the days were passed in training and fatigue duties. We signallers had as usual our own duties to perform in keeping up the daily communications with brigade and divisional hqrs, also with the left and right battalions. The rough winter weather began to merge into the balmy days of spring and this, with the change from trench life and fighting, did us all good. Jimmy Sharp and I during our spare time, on the wander as usual, found a trench of buried cables and at intervals as we followed the route of these, we found where the Germans had dug down to the wires and with an axe had hacked them to pieces before they retreated, to make them useless to us. How thorough they had been in everything pertaining to their successful retreat! On April 17th we were relieved by the 2nd Welsh, and we handed in our signalling equipment and once more prepared for the road. Marching by way of the villages of Mesnil, Mesnil-le-Petit and Curchy, we came again to Rosieres, a distance of 14 miles. The road had been a rough one and we were glad of billets for the night. During this day's march we were struck by the wanton destruction indulged in by the enemy, in cutting down nearly all of the fruit trees growing by the way side, as they had retreated. Such destruction could not in any way have been a benefit to them, yet they had sawn them almost through and then pulled them down. In the morning we moved off again, passing through Vauvillers, Framerville and Proyart to Chuignolles, where we settled down in wooden billets fitted up with beds made from wire netting, which to our tired bodies were very comfortable. We had marched 20 miles along bad roads and in pouring rain, and were sore and tired. The usual parades were here again very much in vogue. We had the opportunity of Church Parade on the 22nd, and I attended Church of England service in the Church Army tent where the singing and the voice of the padre, was often interrupted by the booming of big guns in the distance, and the wailing sound of giant shells as they sailed high overhead.

In the morning, the signal section commenced visual communication with divisional headquarters. Our station, which acted as the connecting link, as it were, between brigade and division, was situated on some rising ground outside the little village of Chuignes. From 8.30 in the morning until 9pm, we were busily engaged doing the work which ordinarily was done by telephone and despatch riders. We used heliographs, flags, and lamps which were used as circumstances demanded, while we had binoculars and telescopes, with which to read answering signals, and found the work very interesting. How far division were away we never could tell exactly as their signals were always read through glasses. I had charge of the second relief of men, and we had had no less than 33 messages during our first spell of duty. The smartness of our signallers at visual work, enabled these messages to be dealt with safely and correctly and the station was warmly complimented by the Divnl Sig Officer on its efficiency. This work was continued for some days, and there were anything from 50 to 130 messages to be handled each day. My duty as N.C.O. in charge, consisted mainly of stamping, checking, and filing messages, as they were received or sent, and supervising generally. I must say great credit was due to the clever set of signallers who worked with me, and made everything pass off very well. We were rather fortunate in having a good deal of leisure at this time which was spent mostly in games and athletics generally. Football was perhaps the most popular of the games, and we had a very fair regimental team, who, meeting the 10th Glosters on a late date in April, beat them comfortably by 3 goals to 1, and a few days afterwards accounted for the team of the 1st Glosters, in the first round of the divisional cup, with a score of 2–0.

Particular attention was now being paid to our clothing and accoutrements. Every piece of brass and metal of our equipment had to be polished to perfection, for we were now part of what was known as the 'Iron Corps'. This was fully composed of a crack French Division, the Guards Division and our own (1st Division). Apparently, we were all being kept out of action, as reserves in case of a sudden attack of exceptional dimensions being necessary, in which case the 'Iron Corps' could be brought in fresh and strong. With the exception of parades which sometimes became monotonous, we were having a fairly easy time.

Now and again, we had brigade and divisional schemes, and these we greatly enjoyed, for the reason that they gave us the opportunity seeing over a larger area of country than we otherwise might have done. In addition, there were the regular bathing parades at Chuignes a few miles distant, which always occupied one day for each battalion. On the 7th May the Camerons beat the Divnl A.S.C. in the second round of the divisional cup by 3 goals to 1, and two days later gained a win over the Divnl Artillery team by 1–0.

We had a divisional scheme on the 16th, but as the Camerons had the position of reserve battalion we found little to do, and the day passed off much like a picnic. 'D' coy held their sports on the 18th May, at which I took first prize for the ¼ mile and second for the ½ mile. Next day we bade farewell to Chuignolles – pronounced Schween-olles – and marching by Proyart, down the St Quentin–Amiens road through the village of Lauotte; we arrived at the little country town of Marcelcave. The week following was spent in training, but on Saturday 26th May we heard rumours of a train journey. This seemed to indicate we were going to a new sector, and probably some more fighting.

26
Northwards to Belgium

The battalion paraded that night at 11.30, in full marching order, and with each man carrying his two blankets strapped to the top of his pack. A little incident occurred in connection with a bit of misbehaviour on the part of a few, but for which the whole regiment had to pay in full. Some of the men of 'A' Coy had found a barrel of 'vin blanc' or white wine, and in view of future needs, had filled up the 'dixies' belonging to the cooker with wine instead of water, while not a few had also filled the water bottles they carried. The result was the wine was smelt on parade. The C.O., Sir Thos Erskine Bart., better known to his men as 'the tramp', was furious, and there was considerable delay while the whole regiment was searched for wine. At last we were safely entrained and journeyed towards the coast by way of Abbeville to Etaples, then skirting the shore, we passed through Boulougne and Calais. Turning inland again from the latter town, we came to Hazebrouck, and thence to the village of Godwersvelde. Here, we left the train and had to march to the neighbouring village of Theushook, a distance of 3 miles, but the C.O., remembering the incident of the 'vin blanc' at Marcelcave, took us a roundabout way for a distance of about 10 miles. This was the punishment, and a terrible march it was, weighted down as we were with all our extra kit and blankets, and with a scorching sun above us. It was not surprising that men began to fall out by the roadside, and I never remember seeing the battalion in a more distressed condition. 'The Tramp', mounted on his horse, rode in front, grim and silent, and never offering his men the usual ten minutes rest per hour allowed under marching regulations. Had it not been for the R.S.M., I believe the battalion would have mutinied that evening. Only when he pointed out to the C.O. the unnecessary suffering he was inflicting on us, did we get a rest and then to billets. With two or three others I found myself at a farm, but rather than sleep in outbuildings which were none too clean, we preferred to lie out in the green fields, which during the fine weather we were now having, was much nicer, so we used our waterproof sheets to form little tents or 'bivvys' in the shelter of a hedge, and spent a very enjoyable week in this quiet country spot. Our duties were light, consisting chiefly of easy route marches, and various inspections, while we signallers had as usual some very interesting schemes. On one occasion the whole regiment paraded in light marching order for a route march of 22 kilometres. Near a great lumber camp we halted for dinner – a couple of biscuits and some bully beef we carried in our haversacks – while afterwards we had a swim in a stream that ran conveniently near. Thus refreshed, we set off for camp again, after enjoying our day's outing. On Sunday 10th June, I went with a friend Ed Vanwely to a Catholic Service in the chapel on the top of the Mount des Cats. Arriving early, we were shown over the chapel by some monks from an adjacent monastry, who pointed out to us the marks of German bullets in the panelling of the walls, and explaining that these were made by Germans in 1914, when a number of monks were shot down in front of the altar. I greatly enjoyed my visit to this very interesting place. On the 11th, we left Theushook, and marching by way of Caestre we came to Zuytpene. Here we stayed a few more days, most of us still preferring the green fields, rather than the billets provided, which for the most part were barns and byres. Field training was the general routine each day, but once I went to the 2nd Army School to attend a lecture on a new signalling instrument, the Power Buzzer, and a day or two later went to hear another lecture on a Fullerphone. One day we went out on a signalling scheme taking with us our rations for the day. For our last meal we were threatened with a shortage of milk, but I remedied the defect by going amongst a herd of cows with a tin and obtaining a fresh supply. This was an easy matter as all the cows were milked in the fields, although it took me some time to persuade one to allow me near her. Preparations were now made for a move further north, and we were all full of eagerness after being out of action so long. On June 19th reveille was sounded at 2.30am and by 5 o'clock we had left Zuytpene behind us, and were on the road to Wormhout, which lies on the Dunkirk road, arriving there about 8am. We rested here for the remainder of that day, but were off again by 4.30 next morning, and after another march of 24 kilometres we reached Malo-les-Bains, a little sea-side town north of Dunkirk. The whole battalion was billeted in the 'Hotel Terminus', and the first thing we did, after disposing of our kits, was to rush down to the sea, and have a good swim, which we needed badly and enjoyed thoroughly, after our long march on the dusty roads. That night, we slept in the ballroom of the Casino, which had been partly wrecked by shell fire. We were now within range of enemy artillery, and expecting to go into the battle line at once. The following day, we left Malo-les-Bains and proceeded to a camp near the sea-shore, where the shells went screaming overhead at intervals. The camp was none too safe, as occasionally one landed among the tents and there were a few killed and wounded.

27
The Nieuport Sector

On the 22nd June, we relieved the 2nd Inniskilling Fusiliers in Nieuport Bains. As battalion in support, we were in cellars and were much surprised to find that many of the men we relieved were more or less drunk. Apparently a shell had burst a neighbouring cellar, containing a large store of wine, which had been sealed up by masonry at the outbreak of war, and remained undiscovered until chance, in the guise of a shell, had broken the seal, and exposed the contents of the hidden cellar. Needless to say a guard was placed over the wine at once by our C.O., but the wine proved to be too much of a temptation, and I remember the whole guard was found in a more or less helpless condition next morning. Later the wine was removed under the directions of the Qr Master, but I know that many a bottle of good wine 'vanished', while being carried from the cellar to the waiting transport wagons on the road-side. I was now attached to 'D' Coy as signaller, but as the battalion lay in a very small radius, we kept up communication between Hqrs and companies by orderlies, and 'phones were unnecessary. The situation was meantime fairly quiet, only occasional 'crashes' outside, reminding us that the enemy were in close proximity. On the 24th, I was appointed N.C.O. in charge of the brigade advanced or forward signalling station, working shifts of 12 hours alternately with Cpl Armstrong. This was rather a responsible position for us, and we never knew who might be speaking to us on the 'phones. For instance, on one occasion I answered rather sharply an enquiry from the Brigade Office regarding a certain message, only to be informed later on that I'd been cheeking the

Brigadier General. He must have taken my reply in good part, for I heard no more about the matter. On the 28th June, the Camerons relieved the Black Watch, and I rejoined the battalion in time to accompany them into the left sector of the British line. At this point our left flank touched the sea-shore. The position we occupied, as was proved later, was simply a death-trap, being a triangular shaped piece of land, having a canal at the rear, the sea on the left, and the enemy in front. To reach the front line, we went along an underground passage on the shore, and across the canal by pontoon bridges. Our trenches, cut among the sand dunes, were of little use and afforded a minimum of protection, as the concussion of a single shell was sufficient to obliterate yards of a trench at once. Until the sector was taken over by the British, just prior to our arrival, it had been held in peace and quietness by the Belgians for a long time, and it was freely rumoured, that they had been friendly with the Germans. Events seemed to point to this suspicion being well-founded, as, on the night we entered the trenches, the Black Watch observed signals being sent out in the direction of the German lines, with a lamp from an old lighthouse tower. A Belgian was caught in the act, and shot on the spot as a spy. With the arrival of the British forces the Nieuport sector began to show signs of activity. Artillery fire increased greatly, many heavy guns having been brought up and hidden secretly among the sand-hills by the Royal Marine Artillery. The Germans began to waken up also, and our concrete machine-gun emplacements, one by one were smashed to pieces. The enemy seemed to know to a nicety where everyone of these were situated. In our front line trench, an old pump such as may be found in any farm yard supplied us with good fresh water, and the story was told that the Germans themselves had used it so long as the Belgians were in occupation. One day the poor old pump was subjected to a patient bombardment by the enemy, till in the end the pump tree was dug up altogether, clear testimony that the Germans knew more about our own trenches than was good for our health. Working secretly from our side, we had scores of men from an Australian tunnelling company, busily engaged day and night, in mining the enemy positions, with the object of blowing them up when the right time came. The 1st July was notable for heavy shelling by the Germans, and many of our trenches were levelled, while Battalion hqrs, were destroyed by a shell, and the Signal Officer, Lt McInnes was wounded. Telephone wires were blown to pieces, and I laid a new system of lines between 'D' Coy and the signal office, which by good luck, held out through the continuous bombardment of the night, and also the following day. It was at this time a new gun, the 'Stokes' Mortar was introduced in trench warfare, and although a simple-looking contrivance, it could throw shells at a greater speed than any weapon I had seen excepting machine-guns. At short range it created havoc among trenches, and in practice firing I have seen 16 shells leave the gun before the first one reached the target, 400 yards away. They simply rained shells. About this time too, raids on the enemy lines, by a small party of men, were often carried out with the object of capturing prisoners, from whom valuable information might be obtained. We made a raid without losing any casualties, and brought back a prisoner during the night of July 2nd. In this, we were more successful than the Black Watch who raided on a larger scale the following night. For some days, the men selected had been practising this raid behind the lines. Complete models of the German trenches had been made in the sand and these had been studied by the raiding party till they knew every inch of the ground, and the number of the enemy they would be likely to encounter. The party was under the command of a ranker-officer, who, having both the DCM and the MM to his credit, was anxious to win the MC before going on leave. He was in fact due to go home next day, and had his pass in his pocket when he led his men over the top. In the darkness of night, the raiders arrived in our front line, the men, having laid aside their kilts were wearing khaki 'shorts' instead, and with their faces, hands, and knees blackened as a further disguise. After being away some time, during which our guns 'boxed in the particular section, they attacked within a ring of bursting shell thus preventing any escape, or any help reaching the trapped Germans, they returned with two prisoners. One of these died from his wounds as they reached our trenches, while the other, who tried to escape, was shot before he got a dozen yards away. The raid was therefore abortive, the only good point about it being that the officer gained his Military Cross for bringing his men back without loss. Our spell in the trenches being now at an end, we were relieved on July 5th by the 1st K.R. Rifles of the 3rd Brigade, and marched out to billets in the village of Coxy de Bains, which still retained most of its civilian population. Some of the inhabitants, however, dreading the possible advance of the German army, had very wisely departed, and the houses so left made us very good billets. The day following our arrival, we had the pleasure of a bathe in the sea, and this of course we enjoyed immensely, and so apparently did the jelly-fish, which were much too plentiful and clinging for our comfort, not a few of us suffering severely as a result of their stinging activities. That same night we had cause to be thankful we had got safely out of the trenches. A tremendous bombardment opened up in front of us, and we waited anxiously for 'stand to' orders. The order came soon enough, though we were not called upon to go forward. We learned afterwards that the enemy had made a successful surprise attack on our front and captured half a battalion of Northamptons and as many K.R. Rifles. The bombardment served to destroy the light bridges spanning the canal, which were the only means of retreat from the trenches, and then taking advantage of the tunnels made by the Australians, which they had counter-mined, and simultaneously advancing along the sea-shore while the tide was out, the Germans caught the men in the trenches like rats in a trap. Only a few escaped by swimming the canal, the majority went as prisoners to Germany, while the 'press' at home contrived to report that the regiments concerned 'fought to the last man'. Strange, when our own observing aeroplanes saw the captured men passing through Ostende as prisoners of war. While regretting this serious loss to the division, we were glad to have missed that little affair by a matter of twenty-four hours. The ordinary parades occupied most of our time for a few days, while once or twice we signallers marched to Brigade Headquarters for lectures on a new signalling instrument, the 'Fullerphone'. On the 10th July, the village of Coxy de Bains was heavily shelled by German guns, which caused very extensive damage to the houses and compelling many of the remaining people, who still clung desperately to their homes, to flee for their lives. We were very fortunate ourselves in having no casualties during this shelling, though the bursting explosives which dropped everywhere amongst us, causing great clouds of sand to rise in the air, were quite near enough for our liking. The 14th found us at the village of Idesbalde for a signalling scheme in connection with aeroplanes. This was an experimental scheme, and while we worked with lamps and a great canvas shutter lying flat on the ground, the airman up above responded with a horn similar to those fitted on motor-cars. Next day after attending church parade, we had the experience of being shelled while bathing in the sea. No doubt we had been observed from a point on the coast above Ostende. This cut short our swimming, and with the falling of the first shells there was a scramble for our clothes and shelter, and there was no more bathing that day. On the 16th, I was one of a working party assisting a section of Royal Engineers to lay a buried cable along the banks of a canal. Our time in this little seaside place was now growing short, but while we were expecting to go back into the trenches at Nieuport, there came rumours, that we were going to a secret training camp, the division having been selected for a very difficult task, the nature of which it seemed impossible to guess. How far the rumours proved correct will be shown in the next chapter. We awaited the first move with curiosity, not unmixed with trepidation, but this was natural, as these were times when no one knew what tomorrow had in store for us. The 17th found us again on the march and after covering a distance of 15 kilometres we reached a place called Ghyvelde, and here we stayed in tents for the night, or rather I ought to say till 3 o'clock in the morning. Leaving Ghyvelde, we marched through a level, sparsely populated countryside, and for the most part our road lay along the banks of the canals, which, with the strings of barges laden with coal and merchandise sailing along them, are a distinguishing feature of northern Belgium. The little hamlets we passed, with their red, tile-roofed houses, were very picturesque.

28

Clipon Camp

Halting about 11 o'clock, we sat down on the banks of a canal, and had our dinner, while rain fell heavily, and our only shelter was the ground-sheets we always carried with us. The second stage, of our journey that day, saw us heading once more for the sand-dunes and the sea and in the afternoon we came to the straggling village of Loon Plage, a distance of 27 kilometres from our starting point that morning. Beyond Loon Plage, and close to the sea shore we came to an encampment recently erected for our reception, and we were all glad to lie down and rest in the tents. The following day we rested and had also an enjoyable swim in the sea. The sea bath became a regular daily ritual, and every morning we scampered down the soft sand and right into the water like a lot of schoolboys. The sea was at our door so to speak, and there was no necessity to dress. We just got out from our blankets and went right into it and had a good swim, while many a day we made two or three journeys to the water. We were encouraged to spend as much time there as possible, as our next battle promised to be partly of a naval character. At least, we had that idea, though as yet we knew very little about our immediate future, or why we had been brought to such an out-of-the-way place as Clipon Camp. For the present we were enjoying ourselves like a Sunday-school trip at the sea-side, many miles removed from the danger zone of the battle area, where we could rest peaceably by night. Our camp, situated as it was among sand hills was dry and clean, but we found the drilling and the marching among the soft, fine, sand very hard, and very tiring work, and our legs did ache, but as time went on, we got accustomed to everything that at first was new and strange to us. We had generally plenty of leisure too, and indulged in many sports during the afternoons. Very soon we were in as hard and fit condition as men could well be, the sun, the sea, and the sand all contributing to our fresh and bronzed appearance, while the health of the regiment greatly benefited by our sojourn at Clipon. A new item in the daily training introduced here, and the use of which puzzled us greatly at first, was the 'obstacle course'. We were sent over this course at any odd time of the day which made us wonder what on earth could be the reason for so much climbing and running. We did have some fun with it all, however. It was the toughest course I have ever seen, and is well worth describing. To begin with, there were one or two ordinary jumps both 'high' and 'long', between each of which lay short stretches of soft sand; then up some sloping slippery planks which were more than we could manage at first, then a sudden drop of a dozen feet, another rush across sand, and there were ropes to climb and a bar to tumble over, some more of that deep, dry, sand to negotiate, and finall, a 9 feet wall, which offered no foothold, to climb over. This bare, blank wall, after exerting ourselves so much at the other obstacles, was indeed a 'poser', and few, for a time at any rate could master. With constant practice, however, the course became easier to most of us though there were some who never could get over those obstacles. Later we began to do it carrying our equipment, though any who were not sound in wind and limb felt it very severely. For some time each day was a counterpart of the preceding one, and our mode of training changed but little. Day by day we had the same sort of schemes, the route marches, swimming and 'physical jerks'. The weather became very unsettled, and rain fell almost every day. Many and varied were the rumours, and conjectures regarding our ultimate object in being brought to this lonely camp; we seemed cut off from the remainder of the British forces, and, puzzle our brains as we might, we could arrive at no clear solution to the problem. One day, however, during a signalling parade, our officer gathered the section around him, and told us the reason we had come to this strange, out-of-the-way camp. Of course we were all attention as he told us we were expected, when the right time came, to make a forced landing at Ostend. This indeed was exciting news for us, but the strange camp by the sea, the obstacle courses, the sort of 'amphibious training' we were being put through, the hundred and one little things which had puzzled us so much, now became clearer to us – our next entry into battle would be made from the sea. It was for this occasion that the signal officer invited me to take over and be in charge of the telephone lines for the battalion. He was quite frank in expressing his opinion of the dangerous nature of the position, and pointed out that if the contemplated attack came off, I should be one of the first to land. I was duly impressed with what he said, but the job appealed to me, and as for the danger, well we all had that to face. I accepted the position offered on condition that I had free choice of a mate. That being granted I chose for my partner a young chap belonging to Beauly, in the far north of Scotland, who answered to the name of Munro. Up to the present he had not seen much fighting, which was one reason why I selected him, and was no doubt a little bit nervous at first. Later on he became a real 'lion heart', and was not afraid to tackle a job single-handed, and we did have some ticklish things to do, before he and I split partnership after the Armistice; adventures by night that would alone fill a book. On the 8th of July, we were introduced to the greatest secret of all in connection with our camp. This was an exact replica of the sea-wall at Ostend, the same steep, wet, slippery, concrete, the same greasy sea-weed hanging to it; a really marvellous piece of work. The approach to it was a stretch of loose sand of perhaps a hundred yards in length. On our first view, we stared hard at the whole lot, hardly knowing just where we came into the picture, but in a few words the position was explained to us, and we were told we had to practise climbing up the wall – I ought to have said 'practise *running* up the wall', for that, we found, was the only way we could manage to reach the top of this, our latest obstacle. At first glance, yes even after our first try, we thought the feat of surmounting the slippery wall was impossible. It was almost straight up and down. However, we were put to it four at a time, but I cannot remember anyone being successful in mastering it at the first attempt. It was great fun to see fellows get about half way up, carried onwards by their own momentum after a quick rush across the improvised beach in front, then to watch them waver, make a wild attempt to keep their feet on the sloping concrete, and finally to end up in a heap in the sand at the bottom. But inch by inch as it were, we mastered the sea wall of Ostend until the majority of us at any rate could race up it without much trouble, and from now onwards we were taken each day to practise climbing the wall. Then came the task of doing it with full kit, or in fighting order, for as yet we had been practising without any encumbrances, and now with our rifles and equipment it was like beginning all over again. In time, we were masters, and were able to carry up all sorts of things, Lewis-guns, reels of telephone wire, bundles of barbed wire, in short, anything that would be necessary in the real thing at Ostend.

On Saturday the 11th, Clipon Camp was closed for special training, and we were enclosed in a ring fence of barbed wire, no one being allowed to enter or leave without special permission. A guard patrolled the fence to see that no spies came near, and to scrutinise the passports of those who did have to come and go in the course of their duty. The area of land necessary to accommodate the whole of the 1st Division was naturally of immense proportions, and in spite of the guards and the ring fence around us, we were not so much like prisoners as might be supposed, except that there was no personal communication with any outsiders whatever, while as usual all our letters were censored. Our work and training, hard intensive training now, went on as usual, and we had our games and plenty of bathing as before, but we could not now walk to the villages that lay inland. The great camp was silent and secret. On the 14th of August the division was visited by the Commander-in-Chief, Sir D. Haig, who watched us during various phases of our training. Each Sunday found us dressed and with everything

spic-and-span, at Church Parade. Every battalion had its 'Padre' in
camp. The party of C of E, men from the Camerons generally
marched to the lines of the 8th Berks, and joined the service there.
Our leisure allowed scope to indulge in games, football especially,
being the favourite, and great was the rivalry between the different
regiments, that between the famous Black Watch and ourselves
being particularly keen. In fact not being satisfied when the
Camerons won both a football match, and a boxing tournament,
the Captain of 'A' Coy, Black Watch challenged the Captain of our
'A' Coy, to a series of games for a wager of 500 francs. The games
included running, jumping, boxing, football, tug-of-war, and
various other items. The challenge was promptly accepted, and the
various matches fought out on different dates, causing great excitement amongst us, but in the end our side won by a substantial
margin of points. As our training proceeded, we were inspected at
intervals by the Brigadier-General, also by General Strickland
commanding the 1st Division, and by Sir Henry Rawlinson
G.O.C. 4th Corps. These inspections were held on the beach,
which proved an ideal parade ground, being firm and level. On
Aug. 27th, 3 British monitors came to anchor in front of the camp,
and about a mile from shore. Often we had stood and watched the
trail of smoke from British battleships far away on the horizon, as
they passed to and fro patrolling the channel, but these were to be
our companions in the great adventure at Ostend, and as such were
of exceptional interest to us. We were given opportunities of going
aboard the ships in small parties, and many of the sailors in turn
paid visits to our camp on the shore. Some of them were taken as
visitors to the trenches, and all were of the opinion on their return,
that life on the ocean wave even in a battleship was preferable to
what we had to go through in the fighting line. Now that these
ships had arrived, plans of their decks were marked out in the sand,
and for some days we practised 'going aboard', each man having a
certain place allotted to him so that we knew exactly our position
when the time came to board the real monitors. Naval officers
assisted and advised in these practices, while we also had rehearsals

in leaving the ships by imaginary gangways, so that we should be familiar with the manner of leaving when we had to do it under fire from enemy batteries.

On the 29th the Camerons met and defeated the 1st Gloucesters in the first round of the divisional tug-of-war championship, and on September 1st, we played the Black Watch at football, the result being a draw without either side scoring. Two days later in the replay we beat them 1–0, much to the disappointment of the 'Watch' who had a fine team and hoped to win the championship. The usual training was still going ahead, while our sea bathing continued, and also our practises over the obstacle course, and the sea wall, while sometimes we had sham battles by night. On the 9th, we had a brigade sports day, when we gained the football championship by beating the 1st Machine Gun Coy 1–0 and also had the satisfaction of defeating our great rivals the Black Watch at tug-of-war. On the 15th, we marched to Divisional Hqrs, to prac- tise 'the landing'. Everything seemed to point to the fact that we were just waiting time for the great attack from sea. About this time the Germans appeared to have found out, or at least were searching for, our secret-camp, and we had visits from enemy aircraft, gener- ally by night. These visits disturbed our peaceful sleep a good deal, and we had several casualties caused by their bombing operations. The aeroplanes in turn were shelled by Belgian anti-aircraft guns, and by our monitors lying close in-shore. We used to go outside and watch the searchlights flashing over the sky in the search for the invaders, and then having 'picked up' a plane, endeavour to keep it in the light while the guns tried to bring it down. One chap in a tent near to mine owed his life to being a spectator one night when all was quiet and he returned to his bed, he found a shell-case had passed clean through his overcoat which he had folded up and used as a pillow. On the 19th we met the 19th Belgian Regiment in a football match, and were beaten 2–1 which surprised us, but we had to give credit to the 'Belgiques' for having a really smart team. They were accompanied by their bugle band, and it was a musical treat to hear it play. A few days later the Camerons met the 2nd

Munster Fusiliers in the final of the tug-of-war championship. This had been long looked forward to as the tit-bit of all our sports meetings and there were thousands gathered to see what proved to be a most thrilling contest. In the previous year the same regiments had met in the final at Marcelcave, where the Munsters had won through using a 'lock' on the rope. Our team had vowed to have their revenge, and now the same teams had fought their way into the final again. This time all 'locks' were barred and the whole division was interested. In build, the personnel of the Irish team seemed superior, both in height and weight. Both teams lined up on the field in grim determination, each man trained to the last ounce of fitness and an exciting struggle was assured. It was to be an 'all over' pull, and for what seemed a long time the two teams heaved and strained at the rope. Our coach, 'Busty' Saunders, had all along paced quietly up and down speaking quietly to his team, easily the coolest man on the field. At the end of 11 minutes the weight and strength of the Munsters had dragged all our men over the line except the 'anchor' and he was perilously near the fatal line. To the spectators it seemed we were beaten but now at a simple gesture from their coach, the Camerons turned on the rope, and in 15 seconds the Munsters were dragged the full length of the football ground, four of their men being picked up in a fainting condition. The supporters of the Camerons went almost wild with excitement. It seemed a miracle had happened. Actually it had been a triumph of training and tactics, and the team was warmly congratulated by General Strickland who was present to see the great match.

Our days at Clipon Camp were now numbered. The inland push of our forces at Passchendale and in the direction of the town of Roullers was not as successful as expected, and the attack on Ostend from the sea was abandoned. Perhaps it was lucky for us that it was so, yet I sometimes think a glorious page would have been added to history had the landing been carried out. We had now been in this camp, and away from all fighting for three months, and had spent a pleasant time among the sand-dunes.

During the remaining days we spent as much time as possible bathing in the sea; where all along we had spent our happiest hours plunging in the rolling billows as the tide came thundering in, but now we were required in action and with many regrets we left Le Clipon Camp.

29
Home on leave

On Sunday, 21st October, the battalion formed up for the last time on the sea-side, and wondering what the future had in store for us, we took to the road once more, proceeding to the village of Arneke which lay a distance of 26 kilometres from the site of our old camp. On the following day, we moved again to Eringham, and stayed in billets there for a few days. From there we marched to more billets, near the town of Wormhout. In the town lay a divisional headquarters, attached to which was a cinema, and many of us went there for an evening's recreation. It was seldom that men of a line regiment had such chances of entertainment. On the 29th my name appeared in orders as one of a party to proceed home on ten days leave. Leaving the village of Herzeele, we journeyed by motor-lorry to Poperinghe, which was the 'railhead' for the district and from whence departed all leave trains. The little town presented an animated appearance, men of all regiments gathering here en route for home.

In the streets were to be met slouch-hatted Anzacs, tall, soldierly-looking Guardsmen, men whose distinct brogue pronounced them Irish, kilted Scotsmen, and khaki clad-men of the home regiments, but all happy in the thought of getting away from the trenches for a few days. The leave train was due to leave at 1.30am previous to which we paid a visit to the office of the R.T.O. where we drew a certain amount of money. While we waited, much excitement was caused by the appearance of enemy aircraft which bombed the town heavily and were shelled just as determinedly by anti-aircraft batteries, without however having the satisfaction, despite the assistance of powerful searchlights, of bringing to earth the invaders. At last we were all safely on the train and bound for 'Blighty'. Calais was reached at 7.30am and we all repaired to the rest camp provided, billeting in tents all that day, and overnight. Early in the afternoon of October 31st, we sailed for Dover, arriving without adventure, and proceeded to Victoria Station. Here I was lucky enough to overtake my friend Jimmy Monteith who had left the regiment a day in advance of me. I can remember the pair of us going into the Y.M.C.A. hostel at Euston for refreshments, and the surprise we got on being allowed only a certain amount of bread to eat (I think it was two slices each). This wasn't much use to two hungry soldiers, so I gave the 'hostel staff' a surprise in turn, by producing half a loaf from my haversack, and placing it in front of us on the table. After a good meal, a bath, and change, we left St Pancras at 9.15pm and arrived in Carlisle early next morning.

My arrival at home was quite unexpected, and caused a deal of surprise. I was, of course, very glad to be back again after an absence of 16 months and there was much to tell the folks left behind in the village. I spent a very busy, very tiring, week visiting friends in the district, and the days passed all too quickly. Soon my time was up and once more I had to leave for France and all the uncertainties of the battlefield. I cannot say that I had any fear of going back again; I had always been confident that I'd see it through somehow or other. On November 9th I left Carlisle, and arrived early next morning at Euston. From there I made my way across busy London to the station of Victoria.

Here, one saw the various moods of people as caused by the coming and going of soldiers. It was at once the venue of hopes and fears, of joys and tears. Hopes and smiles for those safely home, fears and tears for those departing. Victoria was the last barrier, the dividing line, where men left wives, mothers, sweethearts, and kiddies, where last, fond, farewells were given, and women wept unrestrainedly. Having breakfasted, I joined the boat-train at 8 o'clock, and after a pleasant run through the south-eastern counties, arrived at Dover, crossing over again to Calais the same afternoon. On our arrival, for there were many of us, we were all marched up the hill to the rest camp again for the night. Here I found Jimmy Monteith and Sgt Walker of the signallers, also a few more of our own regiment. After a night in the canvas encampment, we entrained for Poperinghe the following morning, and reached the railhead after a long weary journey made more tedious I believe by the thought that every mile brought us nearer the terrible line of battle. At Poperinghe, we spent another night at the 1st Divisional Camp.

30

Passchendale

In the morning, we marched forward to 'Dirty Bucket' Camp, and reported to our own battalion headquarters. We found that only the 'details', as we called the few who were always left out of action, storemen, officers' batmen, etc, were in camp there, the battalion having recently left to go into the front line at Passchendale Ridge. At this time 'the Ridge' was the hottest corner of the 'line', and in the last few weeks of desperate fighting, many of our finest regiments had been cut to pieces in the vain attempt to force the enemy back. True there were many minor gains, but the general position had little alteration. 'Fritz' was holding on to the high ground like grim death, and any small advantage we gained had been made at great cost. At Passchendale the gain of an isolated farmstead or a few yards of trench was regarded as an achievement of some merit, so great was the contest for every inch of ground in this sector. The very name of the place was sufficient to cause cold shivers to run down our backs. Little wonder that we congratulated ourselves on missing at least one spell in the trenches. Unfortunately our good luck did not last long, and before we had been two hours in camp, a message was received saying that if either Sgt Walker or myself were returned from leave, we had to proceed to Irish Farm, and join the battalion in readiness to enter the front line. What a reception for men newly back from leave! Straight from our own firesides to this inferno. However, we had no choice in the matter, and we both went forward next morning.

Arrived at Irish Farm, which was the name given to a collection of old ragged tents surrounded by a sea of mud, we found the position so acute, that the regiment was 'standing by', and ready to go into battle at 30 minutes notice. Next morning, just as the piper was playing 'reveille', our camp was bombed by enemy aeroplanes, and artillery also opened out on us. We sought what shelter there was in some old trenches, and as we stood there a piece of shrapnel missed my head by a hairs breadth, and buried itself between my feet in the bottom of the trench. By and by, things quietened down again, but with the heavy rain which fell and being very wet and cold, not to speak of the quagmire in which our camp was situated, we were in a most miserable state. On the night of the 15th November, the Camerons relieved the 2nd Royal Sussex on the left position of the 'Ridge'. Only about half of the regiment went into action as the accommodation was limited. Battalion Hqrs were situated in a captured German 'pill box' at Meetcheele, but this was so small that only the C.O. and the Adjutant, together with two telephone operators, could get inside. The remainder of the hqrs had to take what shelter we could find behind a wall, which was really no shelter at all. This was our first time in action since I took charge of the telephone lines, and I found little or no communication between companies. It seemed impossible in the constant shelling that was going on to keep telephone wires 'through'. Without any help, my partner had been left behind, I knew I had a big task on hand to arrange any lines of communication. I searched around till I found a wire leading to our support company some distance in the rear, and was able to repair this, and keep it in working order. From the support company, contact with brigade headquarters was made with lamp signalling, all contrived so that the enemy could not detect it. The line to the support company was therefore very important, and acted as a sort of back-door through which reserves could be summoned when necessary. The biggest puzzle was the left front company, to which there was no line at all. Having salvaged as much wire as I thought would be required, I commenced to lay a line to 'C' Coy. It was all work in the open and mostly in view of the enemy. Shells and bullets were everywhere and many times I must have been very nearly hit. The ground I had to traverse was a gruesome swamp stinking with dead bodies, and often I sank to the knees in what I thought looked solid ground. Now and then the wire I was laying would go up in the air on being hit with a shell, and then I had to retrace my steps, and repair the damage. My thoughts must have been too much occupied in laying the wire to notice the majority of the shells, for now I sometimes wonder how I managed to get that line out, working all on my own. At the time I thought nothing of it, it just seemed to be all in the day's work. When I finally got out to 'C' Coy, and found the wire was through, then I knew I'd done something worth while. The lives of the men of the left company might depend on that wire to headquarters. Although only a short distance, probably ¾ mile, it had taken me nearly three hours to get there, and I yet had to get back again. After a rest, I set off and on my way back I had the experience of being hunted by shells. They were too near and too exact to be random shots, so I adopted a zig-zag course, and through this and by doubling on my tracks I got safely back, and in this I considered myself more than lucky. Soon after I had left 'C' Coy signal office on my way back, it had been hit with a shell and the two men there, Henderson and Tingle were both badly wounded. Poor Jimmy Henderson died of his wounds, but Tingle recovered and rejoined us later. During our short spell in the line, we suffered enormous losses, and there was a constant stream of stretcher bearers with wounded passing down to the dressing stations in the rear. A large number of German prisoners assisted in the work of carrying. They were big hefty fellows, but meek enough now as prisoners of war, and giving credit where it is due, they did sterling work among our wounded, and were very gentle in their handling of the poor fellows they carried so carefully. Without their help our stretcher men could not have coped with all the casualties, and many more men would have died failing the necessary attention to their wounds. Their job too was a dangerous one. The sector was being literally swept with bullets and shells, and it was not uncommon for a stretcher party to be knocked out while proceeding to the rear with wounded. There were many pathetic scenes regarding these white-faced, blood-stained fighters, which caused lumps to rise in our throats, and made us set our faces in grim determination to have revenge. One of the most pitiful sights, I saw, was that of one of our own men, Gaelic bred and born, who, not being able to speak a word of English, lying on a stretcher badly wounded internally, could not tell us how to ease him in his agony. On our right flank lay the 1st Canadians, this being the first instance during the war that the two 1st Divisions had fought shoulder to shoulder. Like us, the Canadians were losing heavily. Blood and mud were mixing freely on the shell-battered ridges of Passchendale, good men falling as the leaves fall in autumn. Trenches were knocked to pieces, and we lay in any sort of holes in the hope of escaping the hail of high explosives and machine-gun fire. On the night of the 16th November, our second night in the line, the Camerons went over the top and captured two forti-fied farms, held by the enemy, together with 25 prisoners. It was a successful attack carried out under a murderous fire. The farms proved hard nuts to crack and their defenders sheltered in their concrete emplacements caused us many casualties and it was not until we could reach them by bombs through loop holes in their defences that the garrisons gave in, and cried, 'Merci. Kamerad'. What a night of fighting that was for all of us.

I was fortunate during the bombardments in keeping my lines in fairly good condition, but to maintain them meant ceaseless work for me. We had no chance of a meal since we came into the line, just a bit of biscuit from our haversacks, and all the time it had rained and was bitterly cold. Under these awful conditions it was impossible to stay long in the line, and so after 48 hours of hard fighting, we were glad to be relieved by the Black Watch. We trooped wearily out again to the camp at Irish Farm, and here we had a chance to look round and see who had come through alright, and who was missing. It reminded me of the roll-call after Loos. Our ranks were sadly thinned and many good men had made the supreme sacrifice. We left Irish Farm on the 18th, and returned to Dirty Bucket Camp. There, we enjoyed hot baths and clean changes, which we were all sadly in need of, after our experiences in the mud of Passchendale Ridge, though it was long before we were free of the effects of those two terrible days and nights. For my share of the fighting at Passchendale I was recommended for the MM.

Leaving Dirty Bucket Camp, we rejoined the remainder of the battalion then lying at Dambre Camp, and I well remember the men who had been left behind, lining up on each side of the road to see us march in. Probably their motive was to scan the faces in our depleted ranks, as they looked for their own particular friends, who might or might not have returned. We remained in Dambre Camp for three days, while we had a general clean up and a good rest, though on the third day we stood to arms, ready to leave at a moment's notice for the front at Passchendale again. Apparently the Germans were counter-attacking, but luckily we were not called upon as reinforcements. On the 22nd, we packed up and marched to Road Camp near Poperinghe. We stayed here a few days doing only light parades, while on the 24th, we signallers went to the Corp Hqrs, of the Canadians to inspect a gigantic model in clay, of the battlefield at Passchendale Ridge. It was a clever piece of work, and we could trace out all the points that were familiar to us, and in addition could see exactly how 'Jerry' was situated in and behind his lines, everything being faithfully reproduced in miniature on the model. Next day, being Sunday, we had a Church Parade, following which the battalion had a bathing parade. The weather was now very cold, and high winds were prevalent. November 27th, found us on the road once more, as on that date we left Road Camp, and marched to the town of Proven. Here our regiment was quartered in Pompey Camp. Proven was a fairly large town, and showed little signs of war damage. At this time the Hqrs of many and varied detachments were situated in it. It was also a busy rail-head, from which an endless stream of supply columns moved out to the regiments up in front. Our divisional cinema had been set up here, and many of us paid it a visit during our brief stay. Y.M.C.A. huts and Expeditionary Force Canteens were also to be found here, and in these we could obtain those little luxuries, such as chocolate, biscuits, tinned fruit, etc, which we all had a longing for, but which we very seldom had the opportunity of purchasing when anywhere near the front line.

31

In front of Houthulst Forest

While at Proven, we had the first snow of the winter, and it was bitterly cold, so that we were glad to be out of the line. Our duties, generally speaking, were very light. Occasionally, we all had to parade for battalion or ceremonial drill under 'Old Joe', but under his instruction these drills were pleasures rather than work. I had the usual telephone communications to attend to, but once the needful connections were fixed up there was really little to do. It was a contrast to the work in forward areas where shells were for ever creating havoc among wires. All too soon we were again under orders for the front, and at 5 o'clock on the morning of December 3rd, we left Pompey Camp, and entrained at Proven station for

Boesinghe. Arrived at the latter place, we took over some old dug-outs and primitive shelters, which were anything but comfortable residences during frost and snow. We found we had come to relieve French troops, who were holding a position in front of Houthulst Forest.

We were told that the front line we should have to occupy, was not an orderly line of trenches, such as we had been accustomed to, but simply a line of shell holes, while we were specially warned not to move about nor even show ourselves by day, as the enemy had a commanding view of our position from the sloping ground of the forest which they held. Lt Mawbray, our signal officer, gave me a special instruction, that on no account was I to attempt to repair or re-lay telephone wires by day, but to leave all such work till darkness had fallen.

At midnight on the 4th, we relieved the French forces who seemed glad to get out of such a hole. It was, in many respects, a very comical relief, as our fellows, not understanding French very well, found themselves dumped into isolated holes in the inky darkness of night, hardly knowing in what direction the enemy lay, nor at how great a distance from them. As a result, to give one instance, we had two sections of men lost for three days, simply because they dare not show their position by day and when night came they had no sense of direction in the darkness, so that they might as easily have walked into German lines as found their own comrades, had they ventured to move. Eventually, they were discovered by a night patrol in a cold and half-starved condition, due to lack of exercise and food.

Battalion Hqrs took over a captured, loop-holed, building known as a pill-box. This name was given to numberless little squat, concrete, buildings shaped like pill-boxes, built by the Germans, which were almost indestructible. I have seen them dug out of the ground under heavy gun fire, but rarely did a shell succeed in piercing them. In this case however the building appeared to have been an isolated farm building reinforced with concrete to meet the requirements of the enemy, and roomy enough to accommodate a good number of men. It was almost concealed in a hollow though of course 'Jerry' knew all about it – too true, though he had sense to know it was almost useless to bombard it, and contented himself with throwing a shrapnel shell over it at unexpected moments, in the hope of catching someone out of doors. This hidden stronghold rejoiced in the French name of 'Swazonne-des-noeuf-zero-zero', which in plain English is 'Point 6900'. Having dislodged a number of wildly gesticulating Frenchmen from the telephones, we set to work to try and establish communications with our Coy Hqrs, and by daylight had succeeded in getting through to all the stations. The following night I was chosen to accompany Captain Sam McPherson on a tour of investigation. I reckon that was one of the most exciting and dangerous night expeditions I ever had a hand in. Our real object was to try and find out suitable new headquarters for 'D' Coy. Neither of us had ever been in the sector before so that we knew not a yard of the ground we had to traverse. One reason why I went was that if a place was found, I should have wires to lay out to it. Then I had always a good sense of direction by night and could remember what I saw. I could not have had a better companion than Capt McPherson because if not a brilliant soldier, he was at least a brave one. Before starting out we studied the map closely, but once outside in the dark we had to proceed from memory. I'm quite sure we were more than once within enemy lines during our wanderings that night, as we searched for a certain point on the border of the great forest. We picked our way slowly, stepping gingerly among the trees, while the least crackling of a twig underfoot or the swaying of a branch overhead was almost enough to make our hearts cease pulsating. It was a test of nerves and after what seemed hours and hours of walking and scrambling, by which time our legs and hands were torn and bleeding, and after many whispered consultations between us regarding the proper direction, we found the point for which we were hunting, a low-lying building known as Panama House. Not once, since we had left 'C' Coy's Hqrs., had we met a living person and I was thankful when our prowling was completed, and we were safely returned to 'Point 6900'. The next night with the help of Munro and the signal officer, we laid 3,000 yrds of cable to the new Coy, station at Panama Ho. Without much trouble, I found the way from memory, having taken note of various landmarks on the previous double journey. By the time we had finished we were in an awful mess, with floundering through mud and falling into shell holes, which were all over the ground. It had been no easy task in the darkness, and took us a long time to do. In time I had new wires laid to all three front companies, and communication was well maintained to all stations. Through the day I had a good rest, but like the cats I always went out at night, and my work was all done in the dark. Besides looking after the 'live' wires, I laid hundreds of yards along the front line, to act as a guide to men passing from one point to another, and there was no part of the sector I was not familiar with. In my nocturnal wanderings I met with many minor adventures, and my legs still bear scars to prove I often got amongst barbed wire and fell over obstacles in the darkness. Generally the sector was fairly quiet, although frequently long-range guns sent their missiles screaming high over-head, and sometimes an enemy machine-gun would play a rat-tat-tat in the darkness.

All went well until the day we were to be relieved by the Black Watch, when in the afternoon the line to 'D' Coy failed. The signal officer, in his excitement, sent Cpl Mc Donald to me to ask if I would be able to repair it. I remembered the instructions I had got about keeping off the lines in daylight, and Mc Donald understood just as well as I, what such a request meant. 'D' Coy of all compa-nies! To try and reach any coy by day was a big risk, but to go on the line to Panama House was courting death from the German machine-guns, but I think he was surprised when I said 'Tell Mr Mawbray I'll be off in a few minutes'. Mac pointed out the risk, which I understood even better than he but when he saw I meant to go he offered to go also, as did my own mate Munro. I told them there was more chance if I went alone. I knew the ground better than they did, and in any case it was my job. After much argument however I consented to Mc Donald going with me. It seemed to me a hopeless task, and I never expected to go out and get back safely. It was early afternoon when we left Hqrs. carrying only a small telephone and a pair of pliers. I had a pretty good idea from a previous experience where the 'dis' would be, and so taking advantage of all the cover we could, we proceeded on our journey like a pair of scouting Indians. Every minute we expected to be fired at, but apparently we were unnoticed; possibly the enemy, not being used to seeing any movements during the day, were not keeping a very sharp look-out, and so we went cautiously forward keeping low-down to the ground. We were within a few hundred yards of the place where I suspected the break in the line might be found, when suddenly a machine-gun opened fire right in front of us. Fortunately, we were neither of us hit, but at the first rat-tat of the gun we both flattened out on the ground and slid into the most convenient shell-hole. Here we lay for a good while and rested. The most dangerous part of our task began when the Germans observed us, and as we lay in the shelter of the hole, we reckoned up our chances of success. These did not appear very rosy to us, and although the machine-gun had quietened down, we knew that more than one pair of eyes were watching for our re-appearance from that hole. Finally we decided to rush from hole to hole one at a time, and trust to luck. There were numerous holes, and our only chance of repairing the wire, was to find the break before darkness came on. Every time we moved, the guns went rat-tat-tat, and we must have been good sport for those gunners, but the luck was with us, and slowly and surely we made our way forward though how we escaped the bullets is a mystery to me. At last I could see the newly made hole where the bursting shell had destroyed the telephone wire, and cut off the communication to Panama House. One more rush and we had gained the safety of the shell-hole and we crouched in it, and soon had the broken ends of wire connected. Now came the critical moment, and the question 'Would we be through' was foremost in our thoughts as we feverishly attached our 'phone to the wire. Should we fail to get Hqrs or

'D' Coy then all our work, and the risks we had taken, would have been in vain. Anxiously we called up each station in turn, and great was our relief to find our calls answered and the line 'through' once more. We were, of course, by no means out of danger, but rather we occupied a very uncomfortable position. There still remained the task of getting back to 'Point 6900', but in this we were aided by the fast approaching darkness, and in due time arrived safely at headquarters, after the most exciting and dangerous adventure I ever had. My experience at Passchendale was nothing compared to it – and yet neither of us got as much as 'Thank you' for risking our lives to mend the telephone wire. Such is the way of the army; we had only done our duty. However I had the satisfaction of handing over the lines intact to the Black Watch at night. On being relieved, we went along a duck-board track, which in some places was built on trestles to a height of ten feet above the ground on account of the flooded state of the district at this period. The battalion head-quarters were located in a large 'pill-box' named Chaudiere. We were now the regiment in what was known as the position of support, and our company headquarters were widely scattered so that I had an extensive system of wires to attend to, though it was of course more comfortable than being in the front line, and I was able to do the necessary patrolling and repairs in daylight, which in itself was a great advantage.

One Sunday night Jimmy Monteith and I were detailed to take a party of twenty men, and carry up rolls of barbed wire, and bundles of 'trip' wire to Gambetta House, in the front line. Jimmy was senior N.C.O. to me, but being a very unassuming chap he would have me take the lead, while he brought up the rear. All being loaded up we set off along the duck-board track, and what a journey we had. First one and then another would be tangled up in his wire, for the 'trip' wire arranged in large, loose coils was very awkward stuff to carry, and was continually getting among the feet, or being tethered among the woodwork of the duck-boards. At intervals too a man would miss his footing and fall off the track into the mire through which it ran. Then there would come forward from man to man the hoarse whisper 'Halt in front'. In such a case we had to stand impatiently waiting until the unfortunate individual was extricated, and safely placed on the duckboards, and the word came to 'Carry on in front'.

In my opinion, nothing was more trying to the nerves of a working party, than having to stand quite still on an exposed track through some of the trivial mishaps just mentioned, and men were not always easy to handle or pacify in such instances, and the fewer halts the better for everyone concerned. I was therefore glad when we saw the outline of Gambetta House looming in front of us in the darkness, and our stores of wire were safely handed over to the Black Watch. Now that the men got turned for home as it were they were for rushing off down the track, but I got in front and refused to be hurried even though the guns began to get active. After many a trip and fall we got back to Chaudiere without any casualties, though one or two had got a wetting, through falling into shell-holes. These holes were often ten or twelve feet deep and full up at this time with dirty, slimy water. At the bottom of them in many cases could be seen the bodies of dead men and mules, together with parts of ammunition wagons, the whole creating a stench that was rotten, and sickening. The ground was a quagmire, and it was disastrous to fall or step off the duck-board tracks. It was customary at this period to wrap our legs in sandbags to avoid getting so wet, and in this connection a good story was told against Sgt Major Macdonald of 'C' Coy. He was a typical native of the West Highlands and on a certain occasion while his company were going up the line, one of his men had the misfortune to fall from the track and plunge overhead in a hole full of water. When he was fished out, miserable and wet, he was taken before his Sgt Major who said to him, 'For why had ye no your sandbags on your legs? Then ye wad'na ha'e got wet!' During the next few days, which were fairly quiet and uneventful, except for artillery and air-craft activity, I was kept busy in repairing and strengthening the telephone communication from the headquarters at Chaudiere to the outlying company stations. On the 11th December, we were relieved by the 1st Battalion South Wales Borderers, while our own regiment moved further back to Noyon Camp, there taking over the huts vacated by the 1st Kings Royal Rifles. The 1st Brigade was now reserve to the division, with the 2nd Brigade in the line and the 3rd Brigade in support.

At Noyon Camp, we were well behind the battle-line, and our time was occupied in various inspections, also in cleaning up the precincts of the camp. During our leisure we played the 8th Royal Berks at football, and beat them 3–1, repeating our success the following day against Brigade Hqrs with a score of 6–0. A team from our Signal Section was also successful against a Belgian team with a score of 3–1. These games of football were always a welcome means of recreation, and went far to detract our thoughts from what was happening to others who were 'up the line'. At a match between representatives of different regiments, there was sure to be a large number of supporters for both sides, and a great display of enthusiasm. Officers, as well as men, liked to see their own team play and win. One morning while we stayed at Noyon Camp, one of our signallers rushed up to me in a state of great excitement with the news that my name was in the daily orders as having won the Military Medal. Although I was aware of the recommendation in connection with the affair at Passchendale, it was hard to believe anything had come of it.

32
Decorations on the field

The 19th of December was in the nature of a red-letter day for me, that being the date set apart by Maj Gen Strickland for the award of decorations. A selected party of 200 men, from each of the four battalions of the 1st Brigade, marched from their respective camps to a field near Woeston, where they were all drawn up in the form of a hollow square to witness the ceremony. The half-dozen officers and men, who were to be decorated, were lined up inside this formation, while on the opposite side of the square stood a small table on which lay the decorations, and the papers respecting each man to receive an award. With the arrival of the Divisional General the ceremony began. Names were called out by the Brigade Major, and each man in turn advanced across the field. At the table a brief account of the act, for which the decoration was awarded, was read over, then the General pinned on the ribbon, spoke a few words to the recipient and finished by shaking hands. I confess to a deal of nervousness when my turn came, and I could not attempt to describe how I walked across the intervening space to the table, but I can remember the Brigade-Major reading from the papers he held in his hand; 'Military Medal, awarded to no 12768, L/Cpl John Jackson – For conspicuous bravery in laying and maintaining telephone cables singlehanded, under heavy enemy fire at Passchendale Ridge on November 16th 1917'. General Strickland then pinned the little red-white-and-blue ribbon of the Military Medal on my tunic, and as he shook hands, he said to me 'You had a hard job, but you did it damned well'. When all the decorations, which included 2 MCs, 1 DCM and 5 MMs, had been presented the parties marched off the field to their separate camps. I was, naturally, the recipient of many congratulations from all the Signal Section on gaining the distinction.

On the following day, we left Noyon Camp, and took the place of the South Wales Borderers as battalion in support. At Chaudiere, most of my time was occupied in salvaging telephone wire, of which there were miles and miles lying all over the ground. With the help of Munro, we reeled up hundreds of yards for our own use, while a great deal I kept on hand to lay out as a kind of guiding line between the holes or 'posts' forming our front line, there being no recognised front line trenches on this sector. In the darkness, these guiding lines were useful to men going from one point to another. We were now experiencing severe winter weather, and following hard frost, we had two heavy falls of snow. On December

28th, we relieved the 1st Northampton Regiment, and took over our old position in the front line with battalion headquarters again situated at Point 6900. My regular assistant, Munro, had gone on leave, and my partner during this period was a wee chap called Stacey, hailing from Stockton-on-Tees. With a stranger to help me, I was hoping we should have a quiet spell, but as it happened we were hardly settled down till the lines communicating with Panama House were reported broken, and Stacey and I had to go out to mend them.

Since our last turn in the trenches, the lines had been considerably altered so we had to trace them out by hand in the darkness. The ground was in a terrible condition and we waded through many pools of water, and many a muddy patch, before we came to the old German field-gun, standing like a ghostly sentry, which I recognised as a land-mark for 'C' Coys' Hqrs. Arrived at the latter, we learned that Stacey was due to go on leave that very night. When I offered to let him go right back, if he cared to risk the chance of losing his way, he refused to leave me, and said he'd go the rounds with me first. Considering that we were just then about fifty yards away from the enemy outposts, and that any minute might find us shot or taken prisoners, his coolness was surprising, and he showed a good deal of pluck in wishing to finish his work with me. Leaving 'C' Coy, we set off for Panama House which lay some distance to our right, and very soon we came to where the telephone wires diverged, one appearing to pass in front of our outposts, and the other striking to the rear in a slanting direction. The puzzle now was which line would be broken. I decided to take the advanced line myself, and set Stacey off to follow the other, giving him as much information as I could with regard to his direction and destination. For a few minutes, I stood still, listening to the rustling of the bushes as he pushed his way through the undergrowth, till distance at length took him out of my hearing. I was indeed worried and fearful for his safety, for whereas I knew almost every yard of the ground, he was a stranger, and it would be the easiest thing in the world for him to get lost should he by any chance be following the broken wire for it was very dark. The thought of such a happening, on the eve of his going home on leave, and the probability of him falling into enemy hands, worried me greatly. At intervals I listened for the slightest noise from my partner, while I went cautiously along my own length of wire. After a time I came to a 'break', and soon had this put right again. In silence, I continued my way to Panama House, and was indeed glad to find Stacey already there. After a short rest in the little pill box that did duty for a combined Coy Hqrs, and signal station, we made the return journey to Point 6900 without adventure, and in time for Stacey joining the leave party. The following night the wires were again broken, and I went out alone on this the last night of the old year to see if I could repair the damage. It was exactly midnight when I reached 'C' Coy, and in a whisper the Sgt Major, wished me a 'Happy New Year'. The snow was lying deeply, and everything strangely quiet as if under a white shroud as I left the 'centre' company's Hqrs, to follow the lines to the 'right' company at Panama House. Near by lay two German field guns, wrecked by our own artillery, as if to remind me, did I need reminding, that the enemy lay only a few dozen paces away. In the eerie silence I made my way cautiously along, feeling the wire by hand till at length I got to the break. I had almost completed the necessary repairs when some instinct seemed to warn me that someone was approaching. Looking in the direction of the enemy front I could just discern two figures silhouetted against a background of snow, not more than twenty yards away, and apparently coming straight towards me. Situated as I then was between 'the lines', in that well-named place 'No Man's Land', it seemed they could only be an enemy patrol. As usual I carried no rifle, being only armed with the bayonet, so that I was in a pretty hopeless position. In the few seconds that ensued thoughts of many things passed through my mind in rapid succession. 'Would the approaching men be friends or enemies? If the latter, was this to be my exit; had I seen the last of my comrades; would I be shot; or would it mean a prisoner of war in Germany?' To try and run for it would only reveal my presence, and seemed like asking to be shot, so I decided to stand my ground, and trust to luck to escape observation among the few posts and tree stumps that stood around me. By the time I had thought all this the men were only a few feet away, and I was hoping they were going to pass me by, when suddenly they stopped, and one of them, in a cold, level voice, said, 'Who's that?' It was indeed a welcome relief to hear the voice was British, and to find the nocturnal wanderers were men of my own regiment returning from a reconnaissance of the enemy lines. They were as much surprised as I was to meet anyone in that vicinity, but at any rate it was much better to come face to face with friends than with foes, and, after we had exchanged the usual good wishes for a Happy New Year; greetings that were spoken in undertones, they passed on, while I, completing the repairs to the broken telephone wire, proceeded on my lonely rounds of the cables and it was far into the morning when I reached my journey's end at 'Swazonne-des-neouf-zero-zero'.

On the night of January 1st 1918, we were relieved in the front line at Houthulst Forest by the Black Watch, and I was again fortunate in being able to hand over to the incoming regiment, an excellent system of telephonic communication. The Camerons marched back to the old support position at Chaudiere for two days. Our short stay passed very quietly, and I did little, except make a daily tour along the telephone lines to the company stations. The Signal Officer never troubled me much with regard to my work, and I was generally left alone to make the most of the systems we found at the different places we halted at, arranging the laying-out of wire according to my own ideas. Being relieved by the 1st South Wales Borderers on the night of the 4th, we went still further back and spent the night in camp at Woeston. On the journey some of the signallers got lost but found the battalion in the morning before the Kings Royal Rifles took over our camp. From the wood at Woeston we marched still farther away from the front line and went into our old quarters at Noyon Camp near the village of Crombeke. For a few days after this we had a very hard frost, but although cold, it was a nice change to be able to walk on clean hard ground. On the first Sunday after our arrival in camp, we had a church parade, and in the evening a good many of us attended a cinema show in one of the larger huts. The ensuing week passed quietly by without any adventure worthy of note. As part of the brigade in support, we were well out of ordinary gun range, and so far as that was concerned were safe enough, but always we remained ready to move forward at short notice. We cleaned up our equipment, had bathing parades, and various inspections in camp, as well as lectures, on the latest poison gas, by the brigade gas officer. As usual, we still applied much of our leisure to games and athletics, which also served to prevent camp life becoming monotonous. The spell of hard frost had been succeeded by several falls of snow, and then after two or three days had elapsed, the thaw set in, which turned the camp site into a quagmire. One day while the roads and the countryside remained deep in slush, a marathon race for teams of 20 men was organised. There would be fully two hundred of us taking part in the race, and we all ran with our kilts on. Such a crowd was quite capable of making the mud fly on a dirty road, and when we finished we were splashed from head to feet, in fact, we could not have been dirtier, had we rolled along the roads. In spite of that we enjoyed ourselves, though probably the spectators had more to laugh at than the runners who took part in the race, which was won by a team from 'D' Company. On Sunday 13th, we packed up once again and marched along the muddy roads, and returned to the old camp at Woeston Wood. Here again, during the following week, we were chiefly employed in a general clean up of the camp. For my part I took the opportunity of securing a large amount of valuable telephone cable which had been left as they had used it, by the French, who had preceded us in this sector. The tracing out of wires laid out by men of another army was in itself very interesting to me as a linesman, and not a few ingenious devices were displayed by the French engineers, in their methods of wiring. The thaw, which still continued, was being hastened by wild, wet weather and caused large floods, which became so serious as to be a menace to the troops occupying the front line.

33

New positions at Houthulst

We thanked our lucky stars at this time that we were out of the trenches, and fairly comfortable in the wooden huts comprising the camp at Woeston. The 3rd Brigade were having a very bad time up in front, many of their foremost posts being absolutely surrounded by water. The garrisons of these posts could only receive their rations from aeroplanes which dropped food among them. The men themselves were lying in holes partly filled with water, and little or no overhead shelter. Without a doubt it was a very serious position. Further behind, between Point 6900, and the pill-box at Chaudiere, there were lakes of water on the low-lying ground, while even the raised duck-board track was destroyed in places by rushing torrents. We, in the warmth and shelter of our huts, made merry in the evenings as we sat around the stoves, but as the wind howled more shrilly, and the rain beat down on the roof, we often thought of our sister brigade holding the line up in front. Following a week of comparative rest, we left the huts at Woeston Wood, on Jan 20th, and took the place of the Kings Royal Rifles at Chaudiere. We occupied this position for one night only, and our next move brought us back to our old sector in front of Houthulst Forest where we relieved the 1st Northampton Regiment. During the first day I had much trouble with the lines to our left company situated at Islande Post. This was a new position made since our last spell in the line, and was a very uncomfortable place to be in, as shells were continually dropping around it. During the next few days, a great deal of aerial and artillery activity was noticeable on the part of the enemy. Evidently 'Jerry' was getting the wind up over something or other, and the sector was warming up in consequence. We witnessed some rare fights in the air, and on one occasion saw two enemy, and one of our own aeroplanes, come down in a heap that soon burst into flames.

After a period of four days, we were relieved in the front line, by the Black Watch, and from there we moved into the position of support with our headquarters, as usual, in the great pill-box at Chaudiere. During our two days stay here, I transferred the signal office into a smaller pill box near the one we called Chaudiere, finishing off the wiring just in time to hand over to the 16th Highland Light Infantry, who relieved us. In their brigade, the 97th, was the Border battalion of the 'Lonsdales', and as this regiment passed close by on their way to the front line, it was pleasing to one belonging to the district from which they were recruited, to hear the broad Cumberland dialect again. In the darkness, I had no chance to look for old friends. On Sunday 27th, we had arrived once more at Noyon Camp, and here we went in for a good deal of signalling practice. I found there was only one telephone line to attend to here, that being the one which linked us up with brigade headquarters in the village of Westvletern, so as the risk of this wire being out of order was almost negligible I was given charge of a new class of signallers. Each day, for some time we had our lessons in a hut, and around the fire we did all the preliminary work such as learning the Morse alphabet, varying this with lectures on the different signalling instruments in use. As the new signallers began to get a grasp of their work, I gradually brought them to the practical work out of doors. They were a very keen lot, anxious to get on, and as an elementary class they showed promise of making fine signallers. No one troubled us, except the signal officer, who occasionally dropped in to see how we were getting on. I may have been a strict teacher, certainly I allowed no fooling or slacking while at lessons, and consequently the class progressed in rapid fashion, and was a credit to all concerned. On Sunday February 3rd, owing to changes in the army formations, we received the 1st Battalion Loyal North Lancashires into our (1st) Brigade, to the exclusion of the 8th Royal Berkshires. On the occasion of the departure of the latter regiment to take up their new position in the 18th Division, the combined pipers of the Black Watch and Camerons played them out of camp as a token of respect, and while sorry to lose such good comrades as the 'Barks' had always proved themselves to be, we were also glad to welcome such a famous fighting regiment as the '1st Loyals', in their place. Besides their splendid records gained on varied battlefields their credentials included many successes in athletics, and as sportsmen they soon proved their worth and became serious rivals to ourselves and the Black Watch. My time was still fully occupied as instructor to the new class of signallers, and now their work was varied by lessons in flag signalling, using both morse and semaphore methods, in sounder reading, and in lamp work at night. Then they had lectures on the mechanism of telephones and fullerphones. The various parts, and the method of focusing a heliograph for signalling purposes was also taught them. Outside parades were almost impossible at this stage owing to the prevalent wild and wet weather, and so with continuous opportunities available for instruction, the class progressed immensely.

The new year had advanced to the 9th of February, before the battalion left the comfortable Noyon Camp, and moved forward to a new position called Kempton Park. Here, the 2nd Brigade were in the front line, while we of the 1st Brigade took up the position of brigade in support. For many days the battalion did a large amount of salvage work in the vicinity. No article was too big or too small to be passed by, and consequently a huge dump was collected, and in it might have been found a waterbottle or a bayonet, an ammunition limber or a field-gun. Everything was sorted, checked, and finally despatched to the salvage dumps down the line. We found many curious articles, not all British, and saw some gruesome sights in our search of the surrounding district for salvage. On occasions, too, while we stayed at Kempton Park, we assisted the engineers in erecting the familiar little bow-huts of which so many military camps at home consisted. Many thousands of these were now being built, up and down the country, for the accommodation of troops behind the battle area. Work of this sort was a decided change for us, and compared with life in a fire trench where every minute had its dangers and anxieties, the task of fitting sections of huts together appealed to us as a new sort of game, and we went at it with a will. On the 20th we reverted, to our original position as a fighting force, and the battalion took over the trenches held by the 2nd Royal Sussex Regiment in the left half of our new sector. Our 'A' 'B' and 'C' companies were all deployed in the fire bays of the front trenches, while 'D' company acted as reserve and occupied a position situated in what was known as Pheasant Trench. I remember this trench as the place where the largest British dug-out I had ever seen was then being built, and for the bluish, clayey, substance of the earth which was in process of excavation. What this enormous place was being made for I never learned. On the day following our arrival, I went off to trace out the lines to the company stations; an exact knowledge of every telephone wire in use and where it led to being one of my chief studies, as I never could tell at what hour of the day or night I should have to turn out to do repairs. On my way, I mended a wire leading to a place which bore the name of 'The Brewery'. I might add 'the Brewery' was 'dry', and out of action so far as liquid refreshments affected it. The telephone lines seemed to have been laid out in a hurry, and many of them crossed areas that were decidedly exposed to enemy view and rifle fire. In many instances these places, easily seen by the Germans in the daytime, had a rifle trained on them during darkness, from which chance shots were fired at irregular intervals and many a man was knocked out or wounded by coming into the alignment of a fixed rifle. None of the signallers envied my job of going round the lines especially in the darkness, and though in their case there were enough men to relieve them and allow them spells out of the line in turn, there was no such relief for me, and on the register we kept for that purpose, I easily held the record for 'attendances' in the fighting line. Intermittent shelling by the enemy was responsible for many interruptions in our telephonic communications, while on occasions I spent hours during the night testing for faults caused by wear and tear of the wires, which in many cases lay along the ground where they were often trampled upon. At times men, having tripped over one, in a moment of temper would turn and hack it in two, little thinking of the lives they endangered by such ruthless, and wanton destruction. The bursting of shells in dangerous proximity to where I often had to do my work, the woeful whine of these giant explosives, as they hurtled through the air, together with the staccato bark of enemy machine-guns, and the resultant 'ping', 'ping' of bullets, seemed to be a part of my daily (or nightly) programme, and yet through it all I seemed to bear a charmed life, for though many a time I was 'missed by inches', as the saying goes, I never was actually hit. I had a great deal of trouble with the line that ran across a very exposed and open piece of ground to our right front company at Gloster Farm, from our own headquarter station at Norfolk Ho. The problem of maintaining communication with the centre company was effectually solved by resorting to visual signalling. This method was of course seldom applicable owing to enemy observation. In this instance, at Meunier Post, we used lamps and they were a success. We were relieved at Norfolk House on the 24th February by the 1st Loyal North Lancashires, and went into position as battalion in support at Hugles Halles. Our new quarters were a row of concrete dug-outs built into a bank, the only fault to them being that they faced the wrong way, that is, towards the German lines. Originally belonging to the Germans, who made them, these cave-like shelters had been captured by our forces a few months previous. Situated a little to the right of this position lay the road to Poelcappele, and along this could be seen the fragments of a large number of British tanks, which had been shelled and completely wrecked by the enemy guns during the attack in 1917 which had for its objective the important town of Roullers. This had been more or less a failure, and the quantity of scrap-iron that littered the road testified that the tanks in their first serious fight met their match, and were severely battered. All around us in the most unexpected positions were a large number of our own guns, both field and heavy batteries being in evidence. Artillery duels were constantly in operation and when the guns were busy we had always to be on the look-out for gas-shells coming over, as the Germans searched the vicinity with their deadly poison-gas shells in the hope of putting an end to some of our gunners. For two days we stayed in Hugles Halles, during which time I found plenty to do repairing our left company's line leading to Pheasant Trench. On the 26th, we handed over our position to the Black Watch, and went forward into the right half of the sector, our battalion headquarters being formed at Hubner Farm, with the companies A, B, and D, holding the front line, and C Company occupying a position as reserve. The spasmodic activity of the enemy artillery caused havoc among the telephone wires, and gave me a lot of extra work repairing these, but fortunately I was able to do most of it during the day time. On the second day of our spell in the front trenches, I managed to get round all the company lines, the route taking me by way of Winchester Farm, Burns House, and Oxford House. Being an entirely new area for us I had all the wires to trace out and this took me a long time. At night Tingle and I attempted to lay out an alternate route between Winchester Farm and Oxford House by way of Sourd Post, but after struggling with drums of wire amongst swampy ground for the greater part of the night, not to speak of losing our bearings more than once, we had to abandon our plans owing to daylight appearing on the scene. The night brought with it a few adventures, and in our wanderings we stumbled into a derelict aeroplane which gave us a bit of a fright at first. In the blackness of the night we could hardly make out at first what the object was; an aeroplane was about the last thing we thought of finding. Later we were held up by some of our own men, who mistook us for Germans prowling around, and it was lucky for us that they did not attack instead of first challenging us. Wet to the knees, with our hands and legs lacerated and bleeding through coming in contact with barbed wire and other unseen obstacles, and well nigh exhausted with carrying heavy reels of wire, and struggling through swamps and rough undergrowth all night, we were thankful to get safely back to Hubner Farm. In a way, it was fortunate that we did not succeed in our efforts to lay the new route completely, as Oxford House was blown to smithereens by the Germans during the night, and it is possible we might have been busy in that locality when the disaster took place, had our plans not been upset by the existing circumstances. On the 28th, we removed from the front line trenches, and returned to Hugles Halles in place of the Black Watch. While in this position, I had an easy time spending most of the day on the wires leading to Pheasant Trench, and Marine View, where two of our companies were stationed. The sector was comparatively quiet for two or three days, and nothing very exciting happened. On the 2nd of March we transferred from the concrete shelters at Hugles Halles to our old position on the left, with headquarters again at Norfolk House. Here we relieved the Loyal North Lancs, who moved back to the place we had vacated. The weather at this time was cold and severe, with high winds and showers of snow prevailing. During this our last spell in the Norfolk House area, the Black Watch carried out a bombing raid at Moray House, a point immediately opposite our lines. I was out among the wires as usual when the fun commenced about midnight on this Sunday evening, and so I stayed among the guns while the bombardment continued. The ruddy glare from the mouths of the guns, which lighted up the surrounding district each time the batteries fired, followed by the roar and crash of bursting shells was something to see, hear, and always remember.

These bombing raids were becoming an almost nightly programme for our men in some part of the line, or other, and as they were always unexpected, they must have struck fear into the hearts of the enemy occupying the front line. A certain point having been chosen as the object to be attacked, and the regiment and artillery concerned been made acquainted with it, at a given time previously arranged (and this question of time was of vital importance), the guns of a sector would all open concentrated fire with the object of keeping isolated, the position being raided. At the same moment our forces, perhaps twenty or thirty strong, would go over the top and attack the Germans. Walled in as it were by our barrage fire, this denied them any hope of reinforcements, and allowed them small chance of escape from the trap. So accurate was the artillery, that it was rarely our own men suffered from its fire, and after a short hand-to-hand fight invariably made the Germans cry 'Merci Kamerad', and brought some prisoners back. On this occasion through simultaneous raids on our left and right it was a lively time.

34
The Pigeon school

On the 4th of March, the Camerons were relieved by the 1st Glosters, and marched away from the trenches to Caribou Camp, which lay on the Poperinghe road. Then, from a place called Battle to Elverdinghe, we were treated to a ride on a miniature railway laid over a very uneven track. The string of small wagons, which formed the train jolted so terribly that our internals were nearly shaken out, but we agreed it was quicker and an easier way of travelling than marching along the rough roads. As usual, on our arrival at a new camp, we had a round of inspections during the first day or two, but even the annoyance, these petty inspections caused us, was a change from the monotony of trench life. With the welcome improvement in the weather, which now occurred we took more interest in a general clean-up of our belongings. On the 8th I was rather surprised to find my name in orders to go on a pigeon-flying course. The signal officer gave me to understand I was only being sent to the pigeon course as a sort of holiday after having had such a continuous rough time of it up in the line, and there is no doubt the rest and change of the next few days did me a lot of good. The party proceeding on the course included 8 Camerons, among whom was my old pal Jimmy Sharp, 4 Loyal North Lancs, 2 Artillerymen and 1 from the 1st Machine Gun Corps. From our quarters at Caribou Camp we marched to a place called Siege Junction, and from that point, a motor lorry conveyed us to Watou, a quiet little country village far removed from the fighting area. For a billet we had an old barn, and having brought our blankets with us, we were able to make ourselves pretty comfortable among the straw which served us for beds. We had our own cooking to do, each of us taking our turn as 'chef'. The first day, we were taken to the pigeon loft, and were given lectures on 'homing birds', also being shown the method of rolling messages, and affixing them, after being put into small aluminium cases, to the legs of the pigeons. Later, we were allowed to handle the birds, which were quite tame. Under the charge of experienced 'pigeon flyers' the birds had become very highly trained, and it was a fine sight to see them let out for exercise each morning, and to note how they understood and obeyed the signals, made by whistling, of the man who looked after them. After we got accustomed to 'flying' the pigeons we were allowed to take them in their baskets for long distances and then, after writing out practice messages, we attached them to the birds, liberated them, and then having seen them safely off in the direction of 'home', we strolled leisurely back to the 'pigeon loft'. It will be seen that our duties were light and easy, and for a week we all spent a very enjoyable time, while the weather was all that could be desired.

Unfortunately for us, pigeon courses do not continue for ever, and it was with many regrets we made way for a new class, and boarded the motor lorry which took us back to the regiment, by way of Poperinghe and Peselhoek.

35

Langemarck Sector

On the evening of our arrival at Caribou Camp, almost all the regiment attended a concert given by our divisional concert party. While in the midst of our evening's enjoyment, there came sudden orders to move, and at 10pm we were on the road to the trenches once more. This time we were bound for the Langemarck sector and after a hard, forced march we relieved the Loyal North Lancs, and our battalion headquarters settled down at Souvenir House, an ex-German pill-box. Before morning came, the signal officer, Lt Mawbray asked me if I could manage to transfer 'C' company signal office from a place called Olga to a new position named Imbros. There was of course nothing left for me to do but to try, so after a careful study of the map and making mental notes of distances, and directions; I set off alone to try and find Imbros in the darkness. Added to the difficulties of the darkness was the fact that we were in a strange district, which as yet we had never seen during daylight. Before dawn however, but after many bumps and falls, I had located Imbros which proved to be a roomy new dug-out built out in the open and so cleverly camouflaged that it took me some time to discover the entrance. Returning to Souvenir House, I made ready to lay the necessary cable, and with the assistance of L/Cpl Bob Armstrong commenced to extend the telephone lines from Olga to the new station. The ground was so level and afforded such little cover that we quite expected to be 'spotted' by the enemy before our task was complete. So it happened that we had hardly got started on our journey till the bullets began to whizz and whine all about us. Shortly afterwards I suddenly missed my companion, but on looking back I saw him running as hard as he could go towards an old dug-out. Wondering what could be wrong, for Bob was not the kind that would leave a fellow in the lurch, I laid down the wire and followed him.

In the old shelter, I found him with his tunic off and nursing a wounded arm. He had got a bullet through his right fore-arm, so I fixed him up with his field dressing and a bandage, wished him 'luck' with his 'Blighty' wound and set him off on the way back to the regiment dressing station. I may mention here that he rejoined the battalion when he had recovered from his wound, but very unfortunately he was killed on the day before the Armistice was signed. Bob was one of my best friends, a fine fellow, and one of our leading signallers. I finished laying the wire out to Imbros myself, without any further adventure, and the new signal station was erected there at once. As usual during our sojourn in the line I found plenty to do keeping the communications in order. Now, the whole battle line in France was beginning to liven up, which meant a great deal more shelling and incidentally many more casualties. Bombing raids, both by day and night, continued in ever increasing numbers. Even the 'Jerries' tried to copy our example, and occasionally tried a raid, but generally they got the worst of the deal when it came to hand-to-hand fighting. Any moment we expected a great attack by the enemy, but we did not know where or when the shock would come. The feeling of an impending battle was, however, in the atmosphere and everybody seemed strained and tense, waiting for we hardly knew what. On the 15th, I sorted and labelled the wires leading from Souvenir House to Taube Farm, and the next day went to put the fullerphone in order at Double Cotts, to which we had a connecting line to the Notts and Derbys, a unit of the brigade on our left.

Sunday 17th March was a day notable for very violent shelling, and we were thankful at night to be relieved by the Black Watch. Marching out of the line we now went into reserve at Huddlestone Camp, one of the new camps composed of the wooden bow huts roofed over with corrugated iron. Although coming out of the firing line into a good camp we seemed to have fallen 'out of the frying pan into the fire'. The enemy gunners seemed to know its 'map reference' exactly, and were continually shelling it. We lost several men killed and wounded, and on one occasion had to vacate the camp until the bombardment had subsided. On March 21st, the Germans began their final great attack by an overwhelming blow against the British line at Cambrai, and although so much further north as we were, we did not escape the crashing of shells, as the guns thundered and boomed all along the line in a fierce artillery duel. It was a day not easily forgotten and one that brought its share of disaster to the Camerons at Huddlestone Camp. The bugler had just sounded reveille and as I opened the door of our hut I seemed to feel, rather than hear the 'whizz' of a shell. For one instant I believed it was coming to the doorway I stood at, in another it was past me, and I heard it crash into the hut behind us, followed by the yells of wounded men. Only partly dressed, I ran round to where the shell had struck, and as I pushed open the door of the stricken hut, one of the occupants, an officer's servant fell into my arms. He was clad only in his shirt, and at a glance I saw he was badly wounded, with the blood streaming down his bare legs. I gathered him up with the intention of making for the dressing-station, but had not carried him far when the door of a hut was opened, and our C.O. Col. Methuen appeared still in pyjamas. Seeing the badly wounded man, he said 'Bring him in here', and between us we laid him down on some blankets. Our services were to no avail, however, and the poor fellow, suffering terribly, only lived a little while. The camp was now very much alive after its rude awakening, and other men had come to the assistance of the wounded. Shells were flying everywhere, but so far only one hut had been hit, and inside it had the appearance of a slaughter-house, with the blood of wounded men all over the floor. Of the 15 men who had been sleeping peacefully, 2 lay dead, killed by shock without having stirred from their sleeping pose, 12 others had received terrible wounds in their legs and bodies, and only one man, a scout, came out of the disaster unhurt. It was bad enough to be knocked out in a fight, but to be caught as these poor fellows had been, was too bad. How callous, hardened, and indifferent we had become amongst such scenes may be judged from the fact that after assisting to carry out those wounded men with their lacerated bodies and the 'feel' of their warm blood still on my hands, I could sit down and take my break-fast. The thought of that awful morning upsets me more now than it did then. The period of bombardment died away without inflict-ing any more casualties amongst us, but we were glad when the evening brought orders for us to move into support position at Kempton Park, with headquarters at Cane Post.

We were now in what was called the 'Iron Line', which we regarded in the same light as the enemy did their famous

'Hindenburg Line'. The 'Iron Line' was a specially constructed series of trenches on which much care and labour had been expended. It was designed to hold up the Germans, should their attack be made on this sector, and was in fact the line of final resistance, which in the event of an attack we should have to hold or die defending it. The trenches contained many fine shelters built of concrete, and these were fitted up with beds made of strong wire netting. These when covered with our blankets were very comfortable. At first I had much trouble with the fitting up of the signal office owing to the necessity of fixing my wires to the system of buried cables. Lt Mawbray began to get excited, and said 'I must be fixed up by 2 o'clock'. Sharp and I were working like navvies at those wires, and when the last connection was made I asked in the hearing of the Signal Officer 'What time is it Jimmy?' Sharp pulled out his watch, looked at it, and said, with fine deliberation, '1.57pm'. Mr Mawbray said nothing but he walked away smiling. With the use of so much buried cable, very few wires were exposed here, and I had an easier time than usual. When in bed at night I kept a 'phone lying near my ear, so that I knew all that was going on, and kept in touch with all stations, which puzzled many of the company signallers in the line, who could not understand how I knew so quickly if anything went wrong. In some of the signal offices we had small switch-boards fitted up so that if anything went wrong on one line, a little manipulation of the plugs gave us communication on an alternative line. Often I've heard the men on one station telling a neighbouring office that they were 'dis' to 'so and so'. Knowing all the lines and exchanges so well as I did, it often happened that I could interrupt their conversation and by telling them how to insert their plugs in the board was able, while still lying in bed to get them 'through', and so keep their minds at ease, for naturally nothing worried a signaller so much as knowing he was disconnected from other stations. Indeed, it was a helpless position to be in, and I often wished other positions were as easily worked from a linesman's point of view, as the position we held at Cane Post.

The Black Watch came up, and relieved us about midnight on the 25th, and we crossed over to the right, to take over the front position from the Loyal North Lancs. The Cameron headquarters were again established at the old pill-box called Souvenir House, and for our own convenience Jimmy Sharp and I built a shelter on the lee side of it. With so much interest centred on the huge German offensive in course of operation at Cambrai, the rest of the front was fairly quiet, and there was little movement of any consequence, in the sector we were now holding. Sharp and myself busied about sorting, and labelling telephone wires, and looking after the lines generally. On the 28th, we laid a new line from Souvenir House to 19 Metre Hill, and in the course of our wanderings found the skeleton of a German soldier lying near the Ypres–Staden railway. Probably he had been killed early in '14, as the bones were quite clean and glistened whitely in the sunshine. Only his uniform and his accoutrements, which lay scattered around in fragments, proclaimed the identity of our find as German. On another day, I stumbled across a little wooden cross rudely fashioned from an old box, and which on examination I found had inscribed on it in pencil, which the weather had rendered almost undecipherable, the following words, '260633 Pte. Richardson, 7th Border Regiment.' No date of his death or burial were visible. Here, beneath a simple little cross lay the remains of a brother-Cumbrian 'Killed in action' and hurriedly buried by his comrades. His grave, which had been obliterated by a bursting shell looked so lonely and so desolate that, having found a spade I built the grave up again as neatly as possible. Then with four wooden stakes and some barbed wire I enclosed the little mound of earth, and before we left Souvenir House I found time to erect a stronger cross on which was carved a rough fac-simile of a 'Border' badge, and with the dead soldier's number, rank and name written beneath. It is very probable that his remains would be removed for re-burial in a decent cemetery, when the Burial Companies found his grave, as they certainly would do, after the war ended. We were relieved on the 29th of March, and went into billets at a place called

Canal Bank with headquarters at Fusilier House. This was Easter weekend, and on the Monday, we went to Reigersburg and indulged in the luxury of baths and clean clothes. On our march we passed through the black ruins of the battle-famous town of Ypres. Although within a short distance of this ill-fated town for the last few months, this was the first occasion I had entered it. Some of our old 'Contemptibles' however had known 'Wipers' as it was commonly named, since the first great battle in 1914, when the 'thin line of khaki' held out against the colossal strength of the German army. The Camerons went back to complete their turn of duty in the line on the 2nd of April, and were in support of the Loyal North Lancashires at Cane Post. It proved to be another quiet period and so we had an easy time and were blessed with glorious weather. Up in the air, our airmen kept an ever watchful eye on the enemy, and by day and night we could hear the faint hum of engines as the aircraft soared above us. Occasionally there were sharp bursts of artillery fire which only served to emphasise the tenseness of the nerves and feelings of the opposing forces. Far away to the south the great enemy attack was now in full swing and we began to hear of heavy British losses, of regiments and even divisions being smashed to pieces, with the Germans for ever advancing, and capturing the hastily prepared positions. It seemed that nothing could bar their progress, and we waited anxiously for news, knowing that soon we must take our share of the fighting. Fresh reinforcements were necessary and the 1st Division was strong and seasoned with hard fighting. On the 6th of April, we were relieved by the remnants of the 17th and 19th King's Liverpool Regiment, part of the 30th Division which had suffered severely down at Cambrai. We knew we were bound for the battle-front now.

36

At Givenchy and Esars

We made a hurried exit from the 'Iron Line' at Cane Post, and marched to Bridge Camp near Elverdinghe, and stayed there for two days. Our excitement was now at fever heat, believing we should soon be fighting tooth and nail to keep the Germans back, and on the 8th, we left the Ypres salient behind, and entraining at Peselhoek, we were carried south as far as Chocques. From the rail-head there, we marched to billets at Marles Mines, a typical mining village. Sgt Walker and I stayed in the home of a kindly collier, whose wife made us very comfortable during the short time we were there. Buses whirled us away again in the morning of the 10th and it soon became apparent that our destination had undergone an alteration as, instead of proceeding southwards towards Cambrai; the buses suddenly turned eastwards in the direction of the La Bassee sector, passing Lapugnoy, Bethune, and on to Beuvry. All this district was familiar ground to me, and brought with it memories of the 6th Camerons, of the great fight for Loos, and the old days of 1915. We were told that we should go into billets at Beuvry, but on approaching that village we encountered a heavy bombardment from the enemy, and had to leave the buses in a hurry, and take to the open. The Germans were shelling furiously, for what reason we could not understand, until news came that the Portuguese, who were holding the line at Givenchy had been attacked by the Germans, and before the onslaught of the enemy had left the trenches, and run for their lives. This was the first and only occasion on which the Germans had paid any attention to our allies from Portugal, and after this one experience the 'Pork and Beans' as we had nicknamed them were never seen or heard of in the firing line again. Their flight, however, had left a serious gap in the British line, an opening of which the 'Jerries' were not slow to take advantage, and in the meantime, the gallant 42nd Division of Lancashire Territorials were putting up a great fight and suffering terrible losses, in an effort to hold back the enemy. To go to the aid of the hard-pressed men of Lancashire, the 1st Division was diverted from the road to Cambrai, and thrown into this new battle, the Camerons being detailed to hold the bridges of the La Bassee Canal. There was great excitement expecting every minute we should come in contact with the enemy. Evidently they were suspicious of falling into a trap, for they did not come as far forward as far as they might have done. All around us the guns kept thundering, and the air was full of the smoke from high explosive shells. We had scarcely anything to eat at all that day or the following night, except the emergency biscuits we always carried with us. Our transport section unaware of our sudden call to action had gone astray, and with the prospect of being without rations, we were in a serious predicament, yet black as the outlook appeared to be, we could do nothing but laugh at the thought of the Portuguese bolting from the trenches like rabbits. They had been fine soldiers – till they had to fight, but fighting was something they did not relish. Next day April 11th we moved to the left along the canal, with the headquarters changing positions from Hill 34 in the village of Beuvry, to No 6 Bridge on the La Bassee Canal north-east of Bethune. On our left the line was in the safe keeping of the 3rd Division and although subjected to a murderous shelling from the enemy, they held on to their trenches tenaciously. Meantime, except for the artillery fire, which was also directed upon us we had not come in contact with the German infantry, but we seemed to be just hovering round, watching and waiting to see exactly how the land lay, before going into action. Immediately on the outskirts of our old line, and now in the hands of the enemy, owing to the failure of the Portuguese, lay the little village of Esars. During all the war the line had remain unaltered here since the battle of Givenchy in 1914, at which the redoubtable Mike O'Leary of the Irish Guards won his VC, among the brickfields. Here, in this quite peaceable portion of the line was where the Portuguese troops had been installed, and owing to their carelessness and negligence, the trenches had gone to wreck and ruin, and there were practically no defences at all. It was certainly the weakest part of the line, we had ever been in. With the first enemy attack that scattered the Portuguese, the Germans took possession of Esars while the now terrified French civilians, who had bravely stuck to their homes so long, had to flee for their lives leaving all their belongings behind. Before 'Fritz' could settle down and organise a defence we were rushed in to attack and after a short fierce fight recaptured the village. I shall never forget the sight, as we marched into the grounds of a chateau, of one of our fellows standing at the door of a house, while a barrel of wine stood beside him, from which, with the aid of a large enamel jug and a tin mug, he was dispensing welcome and liberal refreshment (fighting is a thirsty job) to the men passing by. For once, the only time I ever knew it, we were told to choose our own billets and help ourselves to any-thing the houses or shops contained. The owners, poor beggars, would never have an opportunity of regaining any of their household goods, for Esars was fated to be battered to pieces, the same as many other villages of France had been, and so it seemed only sensible that we should make use of anything there was, while we had the chance. Four of us, including the signalling sergeant, claimed a comfortable house as a billet and I volunteered to act as cook while we were there. With the exception of bread we refused our army rations, as there was a good supply of food in the house. In a field adjoining our billet was a large number of poultry, and as eggs were a luxury we took good care that we gathered them all in, but hens and eggs got less the longer we stayed, and when we finally left, the scouts killed as many as they could carry away with them. The C.O. had noticed two large pigs running about and these were killed after various efforts, which I would not care to describe, though I might say they met a 'soldier's death' ultimately. The pork was shared among the headquarter sections, and a large roast was handed in to our billet which later made us a very nice dinner. The enemy counter-attacked in force on the night of the 12th but after a stiff fight, they were repulsed, and we left the defence of the village to the 1st Seaforth Highlanders, who had been sent to re-inforce us.

We were glad enough to get into billets again for a rest. It seemed very much out of place to go to bed with our mud-splashed clothes and dirty boots on, but it was on condition that we kept our clothes on that we allowed to go to bed at all, as at any moment the word might come for us to turn out and fight. But through all the roaring of the guns, and the whining and crashing of shells, we were so tired out, that even the tumult outside did not prevent us from having a good sleep, though what the French house-holders would have said could they have seen us lying in marching order among their clean sheets, and covered up with blankets and the best eider-down quilts I do not know. In the morning the artillery continued its activity, but the enemy infantry seemed to have drawn off. In our self-apportioned billet, we four enjoyed ourselves immensely and spent a considerable time in exploring all sorts of nooks and corners in the village. There seemed to be plenty of everything except money, that and jewellery, being about the only articles the villagers would have had time to collect and take with them. There were clothes of the very best, and we took advantage of them to make a complete change of underclothes and some comical sights were on view as a result. Most of us commandeered fine white dress shirts with starched fronts, and cuffs, in the approved French style, while into our packs we stowed other shirts and pyjamas for use some day when out of the line perhaps. Some men unable to get hold of a suit of pyjamas had substituted certain articles of feminine attire, which at a pinch would answer the same purpose. What outfits we could have had, if only we could have been able to take away all the useful articles we saw. As it was however most of them had to be left to join in the ruin that was gradually wrecking Esars.

The fine old church, whose steeple was a land-mark for miles around was being used by the Germans as a mark for their guns, and high explosive shells were playing havoc with its structure. Monster shrapnel shells too, were being thrown over, and these burst high above the village with a 'Gr-r-outch' that scattered their bullet-and-ball-filled cases over a wide area. One of our signallers nosing round inside the church heard a mysterious low buzzing sound, and, suspecting a German trap, came out in a very excited state. Going back with him I found the noise emanated from a 'Jerry' telephone which had been left in a corner with the transmitting key screwed down. After a careful examination to see there were no connecting wires we took the instrument out, and it was added to our store of signalling apparatus. In the rare intervals of quietness that interspersed the protracted bombardment, we were treated to a musical programme, played on the church organ, by one or two really good organists. Almost every house in the village had its cellar, with good supplies of wine, beer, and stout, for wine and beer are to the French country folk, what tea is, as a beverage to the people of England, but I must say, in fairness to the regiment, that in the midst of all the drink on every side, I never saw any man the worse for imbibing too freely. This may seem strange, but is nevertheless true. Our position at Esars was much too dangerous for men to make fools of themselves by drinking. After a day or so however, the Commanding Officer, Lt Col Erskine, learning about the wine etc, to put temptation beyond the reach of his men, ordered the Scout Officer to take the regimental police and destroy all the barrels they could find. In most cases they were successful, but rumours of their movements travelled faster than they, and at one billet were tricked very cutely and in a manner that could only have been devised by the scheming of 'old soldiers', who are as cunning as a she-fox. Arriving at a certain house, in which the police knew for a certainty there was any amount of stout (having had a share of it) they were shown through the billet by a very obliging signaller of the 'old school', who had been specially selected for the purpose, and whose bland and innocent expression and attitude of obliging servility would have deceived Scotland Yard itself. Into the darkest corners of the cellars the guide led them, flung open all cupboards for their inspection but not a drop of stout could they find. 'Seeing is believing' and they had seen nothing, so they departed looking at each other with very a bewildered expression for they knew they had been cleverly duped.

Inside the house the remainder of the conspirators held their sides as they laughed over the success of their trick and the discomfiture of the police. Piled high in the yard, stood a large collection of empty ammunition boxes, and these being lined with tin and consequently water-tight, were convenient receptacles in which to store stout, and had the police troubled to examine the innocent looking boxes they would have made a grand haul. During the remainder of our stay in Esars it was a common sight to see men going into that yard and returning with jugs full of stout in their hands. An idea of how we fared for food, while staying in these houses may be gathered from the following list on the 'menu' for April 13th, a note of which is jotted down in my diary. As 'cook', I can vouch for it being correct.

Breakfast	Chipped potatoes, steak and bacon, fried onions, coffee, bread and butter.
Dinner	Roast chicken, boiled potatoes and carrots, rice pudding, coffee and biscuits, wines, cognac and beer.
Tea	Bacon and eggs, tea, cake and biscuits.
Supper	Coffee, cake, bottled raspberries and cream, followed by a good glass of 'rum punch' as a night-cap.

The pudding for dinner was made on a large scale and contained a half-a-pound of butter (as an experiment) and as the milk-man had not called that morning, Munro went off with a bucket, found a cow grazing in the fields and returned with a bucket-ful of new milk. Our jollifications all took place under almost incessant shell-fire, and although the houses were tumbling about our ears, we had a remarkably small percentage of casualties. Further to our left, in the trenches being so gallantly defended by the 3rd Division, many men were being killed and wounded, and at 'Pont Fixe', quite near to Esars, an A.S.C. ambulance driver belonging to our division gained the Victoria Cross, for bravery in bringing his car full of wounded safely across a bridge and along a road that was being ploughed by shell, and swept by machine-gun fire. The fight was getting hotter every day, but for the most part it was an artillery duel, and the big howitzers were doing terrible damage.

In the early hours of the 15th, we left the village of Esars or what remained of it, and with us as much plunder from the houses, as we could conveniently carry. We finally arrived at Verquin, and had two days rest and while here some of the old hands renewed acquaintance with friends they had made three years before. As Verquin was well removed from the firing line we had a quiet time, and then orders came to go into action once more.

37
The defence of Bethune

From Verquin, we entered the fighting line in front of Givenchy, and here relieved the 4th Kings Own Royal Lancasters of the 55th Division. This time we were in support to the Black Watch, and Loyal North Lancashires, who manned the front trench. Our headquarters in conjunction with those of the 1st Northamptons were established in the cellars of Pont Fixe, most of the regiment also being housed in partly-ruined dwellings and cellars. We were told to be on the 'qui vive' as at 5.30am on the 19th, our guns would commence a terrific bombardment of the enemy position, and we laid down to sleep on the cellar floor thinking of the surprise in store for 'Fritz' in the morning. It was ourselves, however, who got the rude awakening as at 5 o'clock, the Germans themselves opened a devastating fire on our position. In a very short space of time the majority of our own guns were put out of action, which only served to show that the enemy knew too well the location of our field-gun positions. To help to stem the German advance on the Cambrai front, many guns had been moved from this Givenchy sector, and now the loss of so many more through the accuracy of the enemy artillery placed us in a very precarious position.

Meanwhile, on the opposite side of the La Bassee Canal, the ground held by the 3rd Brigade was being subjected to a hail of gas shells, as many as 3,000 being estimated to have been fired by the Germans during the morning. When the bombardment commenced, four of us were sleeping in a partly-wrecked house so we thought it would be safer if we got across to the cellars among the remainder of the signallers. When all had buckled on their equipment and were ready we made a dash for headquarters, and once again I had all the luck and a marvellous escape from injury. As the first of the four men, I had just rounded the corner of a house, when a great shell struck the end of it, and the other three poor fellows were sent flying in different directions.

Sgt Walker was thrown several yards by the force of the explosion, and suffered greatly from shock. Jimmy Monteith was also knocked over and sustained a slight shrapnel wound in the leg. Purdie, another signaller, fared the worst of any, for he was badly crushed by falling masonry, and it was terrible to hear him moaning as he was carried away on a stretcher. He had only recently returned from home in Edinburgh, where, during his short leave, he had got married. His injuries proved fatal and he died a few days later in hospital. As a prominent character in the regiment he was greatly missed in later times. With the coming of daylight, news came that the Germans had succeeded in entering the front line trench and most of 'A' company of the Black Watch had been made prisoners. 'C' company of the Camerons were selected to go and retake the lost trench, and I have seen nothing more daring, no action so cool or so determined during the whole war than the way that body of men went forward in face of a terrible fire. They were strung out in long lines as in skirmishing order and advanced in perfect formation as far as we could see them. Here and there a man flung up his arms and dropping, lay strangely quiet. Others would crumple and crawl away wounded for shelter, but always the gaps in the lines closed up, and the remainder went steadily forward, and once they reached the trench, were not long in routing the enemy. Back in the village of Pont Fixe, things were getting serious with us. The German guns seemed to be having it all their own way, and whole houses were being knocked across the street, while the air was thick with smoke and dust, making it difficult to see more than a few yards. Added to this, was the suffocating smell of gas, and our throats grew parched, as we breathed the tainted atmosphere. We were losing men steadily among the shattered buildings of the village, many of them being buried among the wreckage. A few managed to struggle out of the ruins two days later, but most of them when found were past all human aid. Two men, one a Cameron, the other a Northampton who had evidently crawled into an iron hut for shelter were discovered dead, without any marks whatever upon them having been killed by concussion when a heavy shell had landed near the foundation of the hut. At about 9 o'clock, Sgt Walker was feeling bad, and I urged him to go to the dressing-station, but he did not wish to leave us, and my entreaties were useless until the Signal Officer came around and begged him to go. The effect of the shell that knocked him over in the morning had sickened him and when I placed my hand inside his tunic, I could feel his heart thumping like a sledge-hammer. I offered to see him safely to the dressing-station and taking his arm in mine we set off down the road. Bullets flew across the unsheltered road in scores while shells were crashing everywhere. Neither of us seemed to realise our danger as we kept steadily on. The pace was of necessity a slow one for the sergeant was weak and faint, but how we reached the doctors in safety I do not know. With a parting hand-shake I left him in the care of the medical men, and I think we both realised then that his career in France was finished. He broke down completely and wept, and I myself, hard as I may be was far from being comfortable. The sergeant was sent right home to Inverness and saw no more fighting. I took the precaution of going back by way of a trench, and returned in safety, only to find our officer wounded and in the act of being carried away. I was now the only N.C.O. left with the signal section Lt Mawbray asked if I could carry on, and I said we should do our best, and, smiling wanly as he wished us luck, he too was borne away by the stretcher-bearers. Going down the cellar steps to the signal office, I told the rest of the fellows that we had lost L/C Monteith, wounded, Sgt Walker was shell-shocked, and now Lt Mawbray was wounded. The news came as a thunderbolt to them. Leaving them again I reported the circumstances and the manner in which we were situated to 'Big Jock' as we rather affectionately called the Adjutant. Even in this tight corner, in which we now found ourselves, he still wore his lazy, imperturbable smile and was quite calm under the stress of the bombardment, which still continued. Saluting, I asked for his instructions. 'You're the signallers eh!' he said. 'Well I think you had better make for the open as you'll be soon fighting for your lives'. Rumours had reached headquarters that the Germans had gained an entrance in one end of the village which intensified the already high excitement, and made us think that the next man we met might be a German so we were prepared accordingly, and moved about with rifles ready for instant action. A few seconds in the signal office sufficed to explain the latest developments, while we gathered our traps together quickly. To 'Speedie' Brown, on duty at the fullerphones I handed a 'Mills' bomb with orders to place it among his instruments before he left, should the enemy force us to evacuate the village. The remainder of us picked up our rifles and fixed bayonets. Leading the way I went up the stairway of the cellar, and had just got outside and was in the act of turning the corner of a house when an officer of the Northamptons stepped from a doorway and pressed his revolver against my chest. Evidently, he had heard us coming and made sure in his mind before seeing us that we would be Germans. I suppose I escaped being shot by the proverbial 'hairs breadth' that time; maybe it was just my usual good luck, but at any rate I was thankful he recognised 'a friend' before he could press the trigger. We now hurried out of the village, which was becoming more of a wreck every minute, and took cover in some old trenches which had been dug in 1914, and there we lay, while the enemy kept up a tremendous bombardment. Our own guns, except for a hidden straggler here and there, were out of action and silent. Had the Germans known that only the 1st Division, strung out in a thin line, lay between them and the town of Bethune, they might have made a large and valuable advance which would have endangered all our line down to Cambrai. Any moment we expected to find the 'men in grey' amongst us, as we lay in those old shallow trenches. The barrage fire of the enemy seemed to fall in regular lines, some dozen yards apart, but strange to say our casualties did not appear to be heavy. Shells fell dangerously near us. One landed in the very hole where a sergeant lay which however only dazed him temporarily, while another dropped and burst within a yard of my head as we lay in the field. All day the guns kept at it, and rifles continued to rattle in defence of the village of Pont Fixe. About 7pm after fourteen hours continuous bombardment the artillery quietened down, and we still held on to our position. Later our headquarters moved slightly back to a place called Fanshawe Castle, and here we had to contend with a lot of gas which seemed to hang about the banks of the canal. During the night Munro and I got some of the telephone wires 'through' again to the company stations, and in respect of one company we established visual communication by means of lamps. Neither of us got any rest that night and the loss of both the officer and sergeant of the section threw a lot of extra work and worries upon me, so that for the next five days I had no sleep, and very little to eat, and only the excitement kept me going. The following day 20th April was quiet except for a little gas shelling. Our trenches in front of the village were in a very battered condition, with bits of flesh and bloodstained patches all over the place. Sorting out and re-arranging the telephone wires gave Munro and myself a very busy day, and in the evening I had the distinction of being summoned to a 'council of war' between the C.O., the Adjt, and the captains commanding companies. Col Methuen asked all about the signalling arrangements I had, and during the night accompanied me on a visit to all the stations. With a depleted section of signallers – only four of us out of the original ten now remained at headquarters, we had a very hard time of it, as with two continually out on the lines it left only two to work the instruments, which meant being always on duty. Munro now proved his worth and made me a splendid assistant. He looked after the forward sections and if ever a man deserved recognition for good work it was he. Early on the morning of the 21st the Northamptons made an attack and captured some trenches and took thirteen prisoners. At dawn on the 23rd we were relieved by the 2/5th Lancashire Fusiliers, and marched wearily out to Cambrin where we entrained for Labourse. We were all about exhausted as we took to the road there again and marched to Noeux-les-Mines. Here we were billeted in a school, and now the loss of sleep and the want of food for the past few days made itself felt and I broke down, and laid on the floor of the school for two days with a temperature of 103°. The doctor considered me too ill to be moved, and my mates told me afterwards that during my delirium, I raved about wires and signalling, and fought the battle of Givenchy all over again. When the fever had passed, it did not take me long to regain my usual good health and in a few days was as right as a trivet. I was recommended for promotion as signalling sergeant for my services at Givenchy, but before the recommendation could be put through orders, a draft of N.C.O's, which included two signalling sergeants, joined us from England and as there can only be one sergeant in the signalling section my promotion was knocked on the head by the untimely arrival of this draft. The section wanted to go in a body to the C.O. and protest against the injustice, but I persuaded them that I should be just as much service to them as their 'linesman' as their new senior N.C.O. The bitterness of the section remained directed against the new sergeant as long as he was with us, for they regarded him as an interloper, and he never succeeded in winning their confidence.

Through the heroic defence of the 1st Brigade at Pont Fixe, and astride the La Bassee Canal the front line was held, and the important town of Bethune was saved from the enemy. During the severe fighting a good deal of signalling equipment had been lost or destroyed, and after checking what was left I made out an indent for the various articles we should require, and took it down to the Quarter-Master – Col Michael Yeadon, MC 'Micky' as he was called had the distinction of being the senior Q.M. in the British Army, and incidentally, he was perhaps the most noted character in the regiment. With nearly 40 years service, and more decorations than would hang with convenience on his breast, to his credit, with his mode of walking resembling the strut of a peacock, a little stoutly built man, with a paunch of undoubted proportions that would have done credit to a brewer, his was a figure that would arouse interest in any sphere of life, but I think it was after all his brusque manner of speech which accentuated his comical aspect. To this mighty personage, I went with the indent for signalling articles. When checking the stores it was discovered that a pair of field-glasses were missing, against the number of which I had written 'Destroyed by shell fire'. The explanation might have satisfied anyone, except our Q.M. 'Micky' got his eye on this item at once, and I stood waiting the worst that he could say. It was a rule in the signalling section that the man in charge of glasses must never remove them from his shoulders, where they were suspended by a strap, at any time. In his abrupt way which might have terrified any who did not know him, he turned to me and said, 'Who's been in charge of the section since Lt Mawbray was wounded?' to which I replied 'I was, Sir.' He scratched his chin while he said, 'Um, far too young boy, far too young, too much responsibility'. Everybody was 'boy' to Micky and though I felt like laughing I managed to remain outwardly serious. Then – 'Who was in charge of the glasses that were destroyed by shell?' – 'L/Cpl Ross, Sir', I answered. 'Um', said the Q.M., 'and what happened to Ross, was he killed?' I answered 'No, Sir'. 'What!' yelled Micky, 'Then why the H— wasn't he?' The final question was typical of the 'Irish' that was in him, and I almost laughed outright. In the end, he accepted the indent, and we got our signalling stores replenished. Speaking of our Q.Mr I once had occasion to go to him for a new kilt, and before going, received a valuable hint from an old soldier as to the best method to adopt, if I hoped to be successful in my quest. His advice was to sew all the pleats at the back with an abundance of white thread to make the 'would-be repairs' as conspicuous as possible. 'Micky' hated nothing so much as to see ragged or untidy kilts and rather than replace a tattered garment with a new one, he would chase the offending owner away with orders to 'Go and get it sewed up man.' In due course, I appeared at the Q.M. stores with my kilt well stitched up in the rear. 'Micky' turned me round and round, then said 'I see nothing wrong with your kilt, boy.' At the words my hopes went to zero, till he went on, 'But I'll give you a new one, do you know why'? I pretended ignorance and said 'No Sir'. 'Because you've taken such good care of the old one', said 'Micky'.

38
The signalling school

On May 1st, as representative of our signal section, I went with an advance party of scouts from Noeux-les-Mines, to examine the position occupied by the 2nd Royal Sussex, of the 3rd Brigade, who were holding the line in front of the brick-fields at Cambrin. What a change there was from the time we had left the fighting line, only a few days ago! Where there had been all the turmoil of a fierce fight with an atmosphere so foul, with gas and smoke, that one could scarcely get breath, there was now seeming peace and quietness, which was in keeping with the twittering of birds and the bright warm sunshine of this lovely spring morning. Not a gun spoke as we cautiously took our way along the road, and entered the communication trench near the dressing station which bore the appropriate name of 'Harley Street'. We found the Sussex headquarters, from whence one of their signallers showed me over the telephone wires, and pointed out the company stations. The next day, the Camerons came in and relieved the Royal Sussex, and when we had got settled down, my name appeared in orders to proceed to the

Fourth Army School for an instructors' course of signalling. I believe I was really sent away for a rest as much as anything else. For many months I had never missed a turn in the line, whereas others had been relieved on occasions. In a way, the change was a welcome one, though I was never so content as when at my own work among telephone wires. Cpl Mc Donald took over the linesman's work during my absence, and leaving the trenches I made my way back to our transport lines at the village of Barlin, where I had a good sleep in preparation for my journey. On the morning of the 3rd I left Barlin, and walked to the station at Bruay, where I met L/Cpl Dunkin of the Royal Sussex, who was also bound for the Signal School. It so happened, we were the only two 'scholars' from the 1st Division, which was sufficient reason for us chumming together. Joining an ordinary passenger train at Bruay, we travelled to St Pol. Here, we had to wait some time for a connection, so in the interval, after satisfying the M.P. and the French *gendarme*, that we were not potential deserters as we passed through the station entrance, we stretched our legs in a brisk walk round the town. Later, we took the train again, and, passing through a nice French farming district, travelled via the town of Doullens to Longpre. There, we found we had 10 kilometres to walk to the village of Quesnoy Airanes. We had been practically travelling all day, and were well tired out and ready for billets, when we reached our destination at 8pm. We reported to the school, which occupied the premises of a fine chateau, and I remember the amusement caused by some of the answers I gave to the Orderly Room Sgt. After the usual information, respecting my rank, name and number, had been given, the following dialogue took place between us:

Q	'Which regiment?'	A	'Cameron Highlanders'
Q	'Which battalion?'	A	'1st'
Q	'Which brigade?'	A	'1st'
Q	'Which division?'	A	'1st'
Q	'Which corps?'	A	'1st'
Q	'Which army?'	A	'1st'

As each answer consisted of the same word 1st, the Sgt seemed nonplussed, and as those standing near began to grin a little, no doubt he thought I was pulling his leg especially as I remained quite serious all the time. The foregoing, however, constituted my address, drawn out to its full extent, at that period.

We found the village of Quesnoy Airanes was of the ordinary, poor, tumble-down variety, only too plentiful in the remote districts of Northern France, the nearest town being that of Airanes, with a population of perhaps 5,000. Our billets, strangely enough, were no better than what we were accustomed to when in 'reserve' positions up the line, being for the most part, old, broken-down cottages, few of which had any glass in the windows. Our beds were 'four posters' (four posts), with a stretch of wire netting for mattresses, and ranged side by side to crowd as many men into the rooms as possible. However, it was a change from life in the trenches, but we had plenty of work to do, which called for a good deal of study, although we finished early most afternoons, and were allowed out 'on pass' to Airanes. Pickets were on duty at night, to see that we kept to our billets, and behaved ourselves generally. Two or three paid the penalty for misconduct by being promptly dismissed the school and sent back to their respective regiments. Among these was Dunkin of the Royal Sussex, who was caught out after hours by an officer. Then there was a private of the Dublin Fusiliers who was caught red-handed, so to speak, in an *estaminet* after midnight by the Sgt Major. The *estaminet* was combined with a small shop, and the Irishman, despite the fact that his pockets contained bottles of 'vin blanc', while he had also a fair supply of the same beverage 'on board', with typical native wit, pleaded, 'Sure an' Oi only came in for a bit o' rubber for the mornin' Sorr'. Pat's excuse, however, was not strong enough to prevent him rejoining the Dublins at his earliest convenience. The school was divided into classes, infantry, artillery, and cavalry being separated from each other. We commenced learning signalling from the alphabet upwards, using all the latest methods by flags, lamps, telephones, fuller-phones, heliographs, and wireless. The programme of work was varied daily to prevent monotony, while lectures, on subjects pertaining to signalling, were constantly being given by the teachers. Night signalling by lamps occurred on three nights a week, and after much practice we were able to read messages from lamps miles away without once blinking our eyes. I think we all hated night-work, and after a time, we were allowed to miss it provided we passed a certain test. Of recreation we had plenty, the favourite as usual being football. A knock-out competition was inaugurated, and carried on nearly the whole term, for medals presented by the 'Daily Mail'. I played outside-left for No 3 team of Class 'C', and after many exciting ties we were successful in winning the medals, which were presented to us one night by the school commandant. The winning team was drawn from eleven different regiments as follows:

Goalkeeper	New Zealand Rifles
Right-back	King's Own Royal Lancs
Left-back	Rifle Brigade
Right-half	Manchester Regt
Centre-half	Black Watch
Left-half	Sherwood Foresters
Outside Right	Gordon Hrs
Inside Right	Somerset Regt
Centre	Northumberland Fus.
Inside-left	West Kents
Outside-left	Cameron Hrs

The runners-up were a team of artillery-men. Though not of great monetary value, the plain medal is one of my souvenirs of happy times at the signalling school. In the evenings we had many fine concerts, a number of splendid vocalists and musicians being discovered in the school complement. Near Quesnoy, a detachment of Italian soldiers was quartered, while units of the French army were often passing through the village. One Sunday morning, we were interested spectators of a parade of French soldiers at which a number of decorations were distributed by a

distinguished general attired in a fiery looking uniform, with glit-
tering sword attached. At the conclusion of the ceremony, the
recipients of honours were kissed on both cheeks by the general,
which, though the custom in France, seemed to us a very lady-like
way of thanking a hero.

A little distance from the village on the road to Longpre stood a
French aerodrome, and during our stay 'Jerry' made a number of
attempts to locate it with bombs from the air. At such times we
were none too safe and it reminded us constantly of what was
going on up in the fighting line. These bombing expeditions by the
enemy created terror among the civilians of the village, who took
to the fields for safety. Otherwise, the weeks were passing by pleas-
antly enough for us at the school. There were days when we were
miles away from the school, doing visual signalling, sometimes
lying for hours in a shady patch on the watch for hidden stations,
or a squad of us would go armed with wagon-loads of wire and
telegraph posts and erect a mile or so of telegraph wires as effi-
ciently but much more quickly than men of the Post Office could
do. When the sun was good, we did a lot of work with helios; then
there was the wireless in little more than its infancy. At times, we
had to take our turns in giving our own class a lecture, which I, at
least, thought the hardest and most uncomfortable task of any.
Maps, and map-reading also, were part of our education, while we
were instructed how to build and use switch-boards, and
exchanges. I was given an empty hut one day, which was supposed
to represent a section of a telegraph office, together with a bundle
of wires, several instruments, and a switch-board, and asked to wire
it up according to my own ideas. This was a job to my liking,
though not by any means easy. Two other chaps assisted me and
when we were about finished, the teacher, himself a Post Office
engineer, walked in, asked who was in charge and complimented
us on a piece of exceptional work. He asked me if I was a P.O. man,
but I said 'No, only linesman for the 1st Camerons'.

At the end of the course, we had a full week to sit for exams,
these including every subject in which we had been instructed

excepting wireless. It was a hard time for us all, and I was glad when it was all over. The school broke up on June 17th, and some time later it appeared in battalion orders that I had passed the examinations successfully, and gained an Instructors Certificate. The result was better than even I had expected.

39
Noeux-les-Mines

On June 18th, following the breaking-up of the school at Quesnoy, I left Longpre and proceeded by rail to Abbeville, staying in a rest camp there overnight. A further day's journey, making a large detour, brought me to Etaples on the coast, and after spending a night there, I went forward to Calonne, stayed all night, and had breakfast next morning with some Canadians, and finally arrived at our own divisional detail's camp on the 21st. Next morning I walked into Noeux-les-Mines, learned that the Camerons had just gone into the line, and was placed in charge of the signallers who had been left behind. There was not a great deal for us to do, and one day about a week later I sprained my wrist, really an aggravation of an old sprain sustained during a game of football in 'Clipon Camp'. Being unable to use, or do any drill with, a rifle, I was forced to go 'sick', and was sent to the 141st Field Ambulance. Hospital was the last place I wished to be in, and a sprain did seem a paltry ailment. I was pleased not to be confined to a marquee, and took the opportunity of enjoying long walks, and it was during one of these aimless wanderings, I stumbled on the whereabouts of my brother, who was attached to No 11 Light Railway Coy 'somewhere in France'. It happened one afternoon I was strolling along the light railway track that ran quite near the Field Ambulance, when I came to a tent which was being used as a 'signal box'. After conversing for a few minutes with the man in charge, I asked him if he had any idea where No 11 Coy would be lying. 'Yes' he replied, 'this is part of it'. At this I was very agreeably surprised, and asked him if he knew my brother. He did, and said I should find him in camp in the wood he pointed out to me. Rather excitedly I hurried off to the sparsely-timbered hill that lay to the south of the little village called Mesnil-le-Ruitz, but on enquiry there I found he had been sent to hospital, the same hospital at which I was a patient, suffering from 'trench fever', only the day before. When I got back again to hospital, I learned that he had been evacuated to the Base. However, 'trench fever' was not apparently a serious illness, for a few days later we met while looking on at a football match, he having rejoined his unit in the meantime. While I remained at the Field Ambulance I paid some visits to the little camp of the Rly Coy on the hill, where I could always be sure of a good tea in their cook-house.

My wrist did not seem to make much improvement, although it was well bandaged, put in splints, and massaged morning and night. On July 11th, I was sent to the 1st Canadian Casualty Clearing Station to be x-rayed, but even then the wrist remained a puzzle to the doctors. After more massage and the application of tight bandages I was shortly afterwards returned to the regiment, though the injured wrist never completely regained its former strength.

From Noeux-les-Mines, the battalion continued for some time to do the usual alternate spells in and out of the line in the Cambrin sector. This period, though quiet generally, yet provided its share of excitement and incidents. When coming out of the trenches it was the usual rule that we occupied the same billets per battalion each time, but there was one occasion, unluckily for them, that the Black Watch took our billets and during their first night's occupation the house, which ought to have been the billet for the Cameron signal section, was hit by an enemy shell of heavy calibre, which very unfortunately caused the death of nine men, while we with uncanny luck escaped once again a severe loss. During the same week, while sleeping on the floor of the school-room, two large bombs were dropped by the Germans in the play-ground which made the building fairly rock, and brought a number of tiles and bricks about our ears but made no casualties amongst us. As a precautionary measure, however, we hurriedly gathered up our blankets and spent the remainder of that night and the following night among the 'stooks' of corn in a harvest field. On one occasion while out of the line the battalion went off in strong muster for a practice field-day, and I was left in charge of three of the signallers to keep communication between the regiment and the Orderly Room, in case of a sudden recall for duty in the line, as we never knew when we might be required should the enemy become lively. We chose for our station the lee side of one of the great slag-heaps near the mines which allowed us an uninterrupted view of the district where the regiment was working, and, the conditions being satisfactory, we used helios. During the day 'Jerry' bombarded the town very heavily, the shells coming screaming over the top of the slag-heap on which we sat while we watched the effect, as they burst,through our glasses. One shell went through the corner of our own billet, and later another wrecked the house occupied by the C.O. At intervals, we signalled to the regiment the damage that was being done, and they very wisely stayed away till the enemy guns became quiet again.

While we stayed in this sector, a large sports meeting was held on the race-course at Noeux-les-Mines to decide a number of divisional championships. There, I had the distinction of winning the half-mile championship of the 1st Division after a terrific race against the best of the runners of the 1st, 2nd, and 3rd Brigades, an honour which pleased the 1st Camerons immensely and one that I took pride in winning. Perhaps the greatest event and the outstanding victory of the meeting, however, was the tug-of-war championship of the 1st Corps which was won in masterly style by our wonderfully trained team, against a crack team of artillerymen. The Army Championship now rested between the 1st Camerons and the 1st Seaforths, a tie that unfortunately never took place owing to the event of the Armistice. Our football team as champions of the 1st Division were, at Noeux-les-Mines, challenged to a match by a team from the Lincolnshire Regt, who were champions of their division, the 31st. The match was played one evening in August, and the result was a comfortable win of three goals to one in favour of the Camerons.

The remainder of our stay in this district was uneventful, and at the end of the month, we had left the town of the 'new mines' behind, and travelled southwards to another familiar sector with headquarters in the village of Chuignes. As in our previous sector, not a great deal of fighting, was going on, though daily there was the desultory firing of heavy artillery on both sides, the big guns seeming to growl like dogs chained in their kennels, but ever uttering their warnings as to their capacity for destruction should necessity arise. Daily there was the list, sometimes small, too often large, of casualties. In the warm summer weather men continued to have written against them, those fateful words, 'Killed in action', or 'Wounded and missing'. Farther south the German attack was broken and now the Australians were advancing tirelessly, while on the French front the armies of France and the U.S.A. hammered the 'Bosche' in a very determined fashion.

40

A holiday in Paris

Round about this time, a system of 'Paris' leave had been inaugurated, in the Canadian Forces, for men who had been continuously in action for long periods. This concession had gradually spread to the British regiments, but I was greatly surprised one night when an orderly came and said the Adjutant wanted to see me. Leave was an item furthest from my thoughts but when he asked the question – 'Care to have a few days in Paris Jackson?' I recognised the chance of a lifetime to visit a famous city, and naturally did not require to be asked twice. On the 7th Sept, I, together with another signaller named Scobie, and Stevenson our regimental barber, set off for the railhead. Here we met with men of other regiments, and countries, all happy and excited in view of their visit to the much-talked-of French capital. There was no lack of funds amongst us, as we all drew a good sum of money at the railhead, while I had an extra 'cheque' left over from the time I went to the Signal School. It was perhaps a little beyond its date and I had hard work trying to persuade the fussy old R.T.O. to cash it for me. 'Why do you want all this money?' he asked. 'I'm going on holiday to Paris, Sir', I answered. 'Oh! that's it, is it', said he, 'Well you'll need it all'. That settled it, and I got the money without any more trouble. From the railhead, we travelled down to Calais, and there boarded the passenger train for Paris. It was a long journey, and a slow one, compared with railway travelling at home. Some compensation for the slow speed of the train, however, was obtained in the views of lovely scenery as we made our way through districts that were strange, and for that reason very interesting, to us, and presenting a decided contrast to that part of Northern France which we knew so well. In place of the dreary level of the battle area, with its ruined towns, and its villages, laid waste in the general destruction, with nothing to gaze upon except wreckage, and scenes of desolation, where the ground was seared and cut by trenches, and riven by gaping holes, where shells had found their billets, we now passed through sunny picturesque valleys, with smiling villages whose red, tile-roofed houses nestled in the shadow of the hills, as peaceful in appearance as if they were our own little villages over in England. So we journeyed to the southward, until twinkling lights only denoted the presence of farmsteads in the dusk of evening, and finally came the darkness which obliterated the scenes as we neared our destination. It was very late at night when we reached Paris, and entered the Gare St Lazare. The train seemed to have been full of soldiers, many of whom, like ourselves, were on leave. Outside the station we were met by Canadian motor lorries detailed to convey us to Pipiniere Barracks, in the Place St Augustine, which was then the headquarters of the Canadian Y.M.C.A. Here particulars of every man were tabulated, and we were advised as to the most suitable, and respectable hotels to stay at. Many men elected to go to the British Army and Navy League Club in the Place de la Republique. Five of us, three Camerons and two Royal Engineers were conducted to the Hotel de Malte, situated on the Rue de Richelieu, which branches off from one of the main boulevards.

The Hotel de Malte occupied a very central position, while we found it very comfortable and in the circumstances not too expensive. It was a relief to dump our packs, our rifles and all the miscellaneous paraphernalia of war, we had to bring with us, knowing that for a few days at least we should be able to do without it all. We were glad to find that most of the hotel staff, that we were likely to come in contact with, spoke excellent English, so that we had no difficulty so far as the language was concerned, and, possibly because we were soldiers, they all seemed anxious to do their best for us. On the morning following our arrival, we were early astir and on leaving the hotel, the first object of interest, which took our eye, was the world-famous Eiffel Tower. It was easily recognisable, and we set off to have a closer view of it. Passing along fine, wide streets of clean and well-ordered appearance, possessing many magnificent buildings of great architectural beauty, we came suddenly upon the winding River Seine. A feature of the Seine is the number of fine bridges which span its waters at frequent intervals. Crossing one of these we reached our objective and then, proceeded from the Champ de Mars, to visit Napoleon's Tomb at the Hotel des Invalides. Deciding we had walked far enough for once, we entered a sub-way station with the intention of taking a train back. We required no tickets but when we joined the train we discovered that none of us could remember the nearest sub-way station to the Hotel de Malte. Eventually we lost our direction completely, and finally arrived at a terminus in the south of the city. Going up the steps on to the boulevard we asked a gendarme to direct us to the Rue de Richelieu, but that street was apparently so far away that he did not know of it, and only shook his head in answer to our questions concerning its whereabouts. It was then that one of the R.E's remembered having a street map in his pocket, and with that as our guide we managed to find our way back to the Hotel de Malte, very tired it is true, after our long tramp through the streets. We took no car, bus, nor sub way either; we were not going to risk being lost again. The civilian guests staying at the hotel mixed freely with us and we all had our meals together, though like them we were only allowed a certain amount of food each day, obtainable only on production of the ration tickets with which we were supplied.

When walking along the streets, we who wore kilts seemed to arouse the curiosity of the French people, especially the old folk who would often turn and stare after us as far as they could see us. In the evenings the cafes with their spacious open fronts were to us an unusual and interesting sight. We visited one or two theatres, but as everything was French and we were far from being experts in that language, we did not enjoy ourselves very much. As might be expected, we spent a good deal of time each day in sight-seeing, though of course we took things easy and did not rush about in the vain hope of seeing everything in the few days at our disposal. The Gardens of the Tuilleries, near which our hotel was situated, gained our admiration, and they were indeed beautiful, perfectly arranged, and well tended. We also paid a visit to the 'Arc de Triomphe', a fine structure constituting a magnificent archway, and at the same time a great national monument to the men of the great armies of France's most famous soldier, Napoleon. Erected over the splendid road called the Rue des Armees, it was at the time of our visit to Paris, heavily protected by sandbags to prevent damage from aircraft and the German 'Big Berthas', which were then shelling the French capital from long range. One day, after having tea in 'A corner of Blighty' at 20 Place Vendome, one of the ladies attached to that place took us to view a church which had been hit from a shell from one of these monster guns. It was hard to believe, even accustomed as we were to scenes of destruction, that a gun 70 miles away could have inflicted the damage we saw there. No wonder the inhabitants of Paris were fearful of what wreckage might ultimately be caused in their own city.

At the Army and Navy League Club, conducted tours were arranged daily, and, on payment of certain sums, which varied according to the distance to be traversed, efficient guides were provided, who would take a party wherever they cared to go. Together with two Australians and one New Zealander, we five from the Hotel de Malte completed a party and paid a visit to the Chateau of Malmaison, in the Bois de Boulogne and at one time the home of Napoleon and the Empress Josephine. Our guide in this instance was, strange to say, a young lady from the Orkney Islands who, before the outbreak of war was a school teacher in Edinburgh. Joining up there as a nurse she had become attached to a hospital in Paris, and later transferred as a guide to the League Club. She proved as efficient a leader as though she had been Parisian born, and we spent a very pleasant and interesting afternoon in her company (and in her care). It did seem funny that half a dozen men should be taken about and be dependent on a girl; she paid all the sub-way and car fares on our behalf and attended to things generally. Arrived at the palace we had photos taken, in the grounds, as a group, with our little guide sitting amongst us on the grass. In the chateau itself, we saw a marvellous array of curios associated with Napoleon and Josephine. Included in this collection were handsome pieces of valuable gold plate, and articles of old-fashioned furniture. Also, we saw the Marshal's baton belonging the great soldier, his medal of the Legion of Honour, his sword and uniform. In another room were many articles associated with Napoleon while a prisoner on the island of St Helena, and the plain iron bedstead on which he died. We greatly enjoyed our visit to Malmaison, all credit being due to our 'guide' who found her way about like a native. The photo of the group is a fine memento of a happy outing. We could always spend a pleasant evening at the League Club, where there were good recreation rooms, and where excellent concerts were held each night for the benefit of the troops on leave. We could well have spent a longer holiday in the

Gay City, but our time was restricted and, in due course, we had to pack up our kits, and hunt out our rifles from wardrobes, cupboards etc. A crowded troop train carried us away north-wards from the Gare St Lazare. We had been fortunate in having our holiday, and though we had to return to fighting, we still had the memory of a happy time in a beautiful city.

41

Gassed!

On our return from Paris we found the regiment miles removed from where we had left it, and now in action, fighting shoulder to shoulder with men of the Australian Forces. When we did come up with the Camerons, they were driving back the Germans in front of Arras. Although the town was still under fire, the train, which brought us back, steamed right into the badly damaged station, where, even in the act of detraining, we were received by a salvo of shells which fell in and around the temporary terminus. We found the details of the regiment in some old trenches just in front of the town, and having reported to the orderly room, we settled down amongst them to await the return of the battalion. When the fighters came back from harrying the retreating forces of the enemy, who were now steadily, and decisively, being beaten back all along the line, we all moved into large cellars in the city. These cellars, under what had once been fine shops, protected by strong, sand-bagged defences on the street-front, formed safe and comfortable quarters for large numbers of men. The city of Arras itself, shelled as it was, day after day by the Germans, presented a very ruined appearance. Of the larger towns in France which had been so badly damaged, probably none had suffered so severely as Arras. Its fine old Cathedral a structure of outstanding architectural beauty, was battered down until it resembled little more than a gigantic rubbish heap, only fragments of tottering masonry, which threatened to fall at any moment, remaining to show where the original outline of the great building had been. Likewise, had its streets and its squares been wrecked in the general ruin, while thousands of pounds worth of damage had been inflicted on the dwellings, hotels and shops of the town. Yet, amidst all the destruction, a small percentage of its people still remained, clinging despairingly to what remained of their ill-fated homes through all the fierce battles that had been fought in and around the city. Arras, at the time of our occupation, was the scene of great and ceaseless activity. Regiments of infantry, batteries of artillery, columns of ammunition, and supply wagons, all bound for the fighting area, heavy guns hauled by giant cater- pillar tractors moving up to help in the mighty push, with a corresponding number of tired, mud-covered men, who straggled wearily along the roads, their faces the colour of the earth they had been digging and fighting amongst, and empty wagons returning for more stores, and more ammunition, streamed in and out of the town. Day and night, the cobbled streets resounded with the never- ending tramp of marching men, the clatter of horses' hoofs and the dull heavy rumble of wagon-wheels. While out of action, we were given our usual light training, and on one occasion we were shelled while out manoeuvring in the neighbouring fields, which caused us to disperse hurriedly and seek safety in our cellars. Such spas- modic shelling by the enemy was very annoying. We never could tell when the shelling would break out, and the uncertainty of the time at which it might happen, kept us from venturing far from safety. Even with all our precautions, considerable casualties were caused by these haphazard bombardments, especially when the high explosives were accompanied by gas shells. I remember one night, a party of Canadians coming down the line on their way to England on leave, all obviously happy, and delighted at the prospect of their trip to the 'Old Country'. They enquired of us for the Town Major's office, at which place they would be able to draw money for their journey, and it was while in there that the building was hit by a heavy shell, which killed every man who was in the office. It was a terrible catastrophe, and gives an instance of the uncertain conditions under which we lived, for we never could tell what would happen next, yet we always hoped for the best and endeavoured to keep smiling. If I remember rightly it was only the morning following this episode that I was almost 'caught out' myself by 'Jerry's' artillery. Reveille had just sounded, and I, half-dressed, had mounted the cellar steps to the street for a breath of fresh air. The morning was fine, and seemingly peaceful, with the sun just rising above the house-tops in all its glory and majesty. For a few minutes I stood leaning against a doorway interestedly watching the squabbles of a section of West Indian niggers, who were having their breakfast issued to them, on the far side of the square. In the middle of their humourous wrangling, came the ominous drone of a big shell which struck the building behind them, and caused a great brick wall to collapse with a crash on top of them. Out of the clouds of smoke and dust, could be heard the yells and cries of injured men and I set off across the square to help the unfortunate breakfast party. Unluckily for me, I was not even carrying my gas-helmet, though even if I had been, it is doubtful if I should have had time to adjust it, and before I was half-way across to the niggers a gas shell from 'Jerry' dropped in the square, and I got enough gas to knock me down senseless. The noise of the bursting shells must have brought others to the scene, as I was miles from Arras when I came to, and on my way to a base hospital at Calais, so that I never learned how the poor niggers fared. It turned out that I was but slightly affected by the gas, and after a week in hospital was sent to a base camp. Here, however, I fell sick again and spent another three weeks in hospital. Rest and plenty of good food helped to pull me round again, and I had a fairly enjoyable time in hospital. An incident occurred here which brought into prominence the 'colour' question between blacks and whites. A number of niggers in hospital had become very arrogant, and trouble culminated in a sergeant being stabbed by a nigger. Immediately there was an uproar which ended in the niggers being beaten out of the hospital by angry men armed with posts and spades. The officer in charge of the hospital admitted that it was the most effectual manner of treating the cheeky blacks, and excepting one or two with broken heads, no more niggers were seen in that hospital.

42

Storming the Hindenburg Line

A stay of two or three days in a base camp after leaving hospital, and then I had to prepare for the journey up to the trenches again, and this was destined to be my last journey 'up the line'. Together with scores of other men, some like myself returning from hospital, while others were new reinforcements from home, I journeyed by train from Calais, via Abbeville to Amiens where we had a brief halt. Walking up and down the platform we found two enormous barrels standing side by side along the wall. These we thought were empty until someone kicked them, and discovered they were barrels of wine. In less than no time a trenching tool was drawn, and the head of a barrel burst open, while waterbottles and canteens were hurriedly filled, and the last I saw, as the train steamed away, was the barrel up-ended, and the red wine flowing like streams of blood across the station platform.

From Amiens, we proceeded to St Quentin, thence to Fresnoy le Grande, and on to Bohain, where we joined the first divisional wing in billets. It had been a long weary journey and food had been so scarce that we made a raid at a rail-head store on our way, carrying off with us loaves of bread, whole cheeses and numerous pots of jam. It was now nearing the end of October, and I rejoined the 1st Camerons in time to take part in the great fight for the famous Hindenburg Line. The Germans, driven back gradually all along the front, were concentrating all their strength in men and munitions for a great defensive battle on an almost impregnable line of solid works of concrete. This elaborate system of trenches, protected by murderous looking stretches of barbed-wire, and garrisoned by masses of men in field-grey, who believed it to be an insurmountable obstacle, against which our forces would be hopelessly shattered, was the Hindenburg Line, and in reality it represented Germany's last hope. Should the defences be penetrated, the confusion of the enemy and a wild retreat by their armies was assured. From north to south the armies of the allies were attacking vigourously, slowly but surely the outer defences were giving way against the fierce onslaughts directed upon them by the great Marshal Foch, while hundreds of guns crashed their iron missiles into the enemy lines in a continuous bombardment. We knew no rest, but were always attacking gaining ground steadily, a hill here, a fortified farm there, or a little village, until in our sector we had come in sight of Mons. In the ranks of the 1st Brigade there were still a few of the Old Contemptibles, who had fought at Mons in 1914 and taken part in the memorable retreat from that point, and now, here they were back again after four years of hard life, and fierce fighting. At the beginning of November we had got in touch with what may be described as the 'key' positions of the Hindenburg Line, and immediately in front of us was the fortified village of Droninghem. Separated from us, and protected by the Sambre Canal, it had every appearance of being a hard nut to crack, and it fell to the lot of the Camerons to make the attempt to capture this strong-hold. At dawn on the 7th November the attack on Droninghem commenced to the accompaniment of a hail of devastating artillery fire. Light guns, field guns and heavy batteries poured their shells on Jerry's concrete defences and gun emplacements, while throughout the general pandemonium of noises, could be distinguished the sharp persistent rattle of maxims and lewis guns, which belched forth death and destruction in a storm of bullets. First, and not the least of the obstacles confronting us was the problem of crossing the intervening canal, not by any means a simple matter in the face of enemy machine-gun fire, and his general determined resistance to our advance. Rafts were hastily constructed from empty petrol tins and pieces of timber, and in the grey morning light, we essayed the dangerous crossing. As soon as our object was perceived, the Germans opened a raking fire on us, and took a heavy toll, as rafts were swamped, and wounded men were drowned in the canal. Bullets whined viciously amongst us, but it was a case of 'death or glory', and never did the regiment live up to its motto, 'A Cameron never can yield', better than on that awful morning. The price we paid was heavy, and dear, but we got over in the end. Once across, and reorganised, we directed our attack on the village itself, and with the aid of a brilliant flanking movement, carried out by 'D' company, and a fierce fight with the garrison, we captured Droninghem about noon, wher, in face of desperate counter-attacks from the enemy, we held on determinedly to our gains. Many prisoners fell into our hands together with large quantities of arms and ammunition. When the roll was called our casualties were found to be enormous, and many old friends were no more. It was indeed hard that many of these battle-scarred warriors, heroes every man of them, having come through the entire war, should, in this our last great battle, have their names included in the honoured list of those men 'Killed in action'. Here, I must refer to our chaplain, the Rev. Father Day, surely one of the bravest 'padres' of the war. Through the last days of severe fighting, he was always with us, cheering us on, and setting a grand example of fearlessness. At the crossing of the Sambre Canal, and in our final assault on Droninghem, where he was wounded, he was always in the foreground of battle, when he could have remained in safety with the regimental details. For his bravery and devotion to the battalion, the gallant chaplain was awarded a well deserved Military Cross.

Our own advances, and the news of great victories in other parts of the line, made it clear to us that the enemy was being beaten. His defences were cracking, and continued pressure was bound to bring about the inevitable collapse. The smashing of the formidable Hindenburg Line must have weakened the morale of the German armies considerably, and fresh evidences of their lost hopes were daily forthcoming, in the dejected looking prisoners that fell into our hands. We, ourselves, were going slowly forward, gaining new ground successively, till we got to the large village of Landrecies. Since the fight at Droninghem, we had met with very little resistance, and we realised that at last the enemy was retreating in a demoralised state. How much longer would the great war continue? It was a great question. After fighting so long in trenches on an almost stationary line, where ground was lost and won, and lost and won again, the successes we now experienced put new life into us. Soon, we could see Germany must ask for an armistice if she was to save her beaten armies at all, and the only thing that worried us was how soon would that happen. In our advances, we were taking prisoners in hundreds, tired, and hungry looking men from the Kaiser's proud and boastful armies, who had no more fight left in them, and were glad to put up their hands and cry 'Kamerad' when cornered. Then came the great news in special orders, which brought joy and relief to every man in the battle line, and the world outside.

43

Armistice Day

'Hostilities will cease at 11am, on the 11th November'. Such was the bare wording of the great message given to us in a special order for the day from Army Headquarters. An extract from the Commander's order to the Allied Armies read,

> Hostilities will cease on the whole front, as from November 11th, at eleven o'clock (French time). The allied troops will not, until further orders, go beyond the line reached at that date and at that hour.
>
> (Signed) Jock

The news must have been welcome at home, and in most countries of the world, but no non-combatants could have any idea what the message meant to the men in the trenches. I think we were slow to believe it could really be true after the long years of fighting. It was strange to think, and know, that once more we could move about fully exposed without fear of being shot at. No more would we need to 'duck' our heads down in the trenches, as we'd had to do for so long. The long nerve-wracking suspense was at last ended, and we were glad, but there were too many saddened memories to think of, too many old pals to mourn, friends who gave their all in brave sacrifice for their country, which was sufficient to keep us from going wild with excitement. Instead, there were just quiet congratulations and a good hand-grip, pregnant with well-meaning, between old friends, still to the fore, who had battled side by side in many a fierce fight, and many a stirring escapade. Now, like the panting eager hounds that wait for the reappearance of the fox gone to ground, we waited for the next move, ready to fight, or to follow the disorganised armies of the enemy. All that morning of the 11th November, the guns crashed and battered, with their customary thunderous roar, as if in protest that the end of the war had come, and as though an armistice was the last thing in the world that could happen. Just as in a game of football, which is ended only when the final whistle blows, we fought on to the last minute; till on the stroke of the eleventh hour the sounds of war ceased abruptly, succeeded by the 'Great Silence'. To us, after years of noise, the calm and quietness of that cold, November, day was bewildering, surely it was the strangest day of the whole campaign. Reminiscently, our thoughts flew back over the great adventures of the past years, recalling brave men, who had done their bit, and 'gone west' in the doing of it, and then our musings were cut short, and we came back to realities when someone voiced the question, 'How long will it be till we are back home?' As events proved, we were still a long way from home. Lying between the villages of Landrecies and Mons, it seemed strange that our regiment should 'cease fire' on the identical ground where it first met the enemy forces in 1914. By command, we were not allowed to cross over to the German troops, nor to attempt any conversation, or exchange any signals with them. While we rested here quietly for a few days, our 'late' enemy began preparations for a hurried journey home, and we were part of the forces detailed to see them safely into the 'Fatherland'.

44
A long, long trail

The news of our prospective trip to Germany was exciting enough, even though it meant a long journey in wintry weather. Large forces of cavalry now made their appearance in the vicinity, they to be used as a connecting link, between the retreating Germans and our infantry, which followed a few day's march behind. On November 14th, we had moved to the village called Sars Poitieries, and continuing our march the following day, we came to Grandrieuse, and halted there for the next two days. On the 18th, we took to the road again and a journey of 18 kilometres brought us to the little town of Castillon. A night's rest here, and off we went again, our destination this time being Laneffe a village 20 kilometres further to the north-east. This constant marching day after day, following closely on the strenuous fighting prior to the Armistice was terribly hard on us, the roads, after the passage of the heavy German artillery and other weighty machinery of war, were in a fearful state, which was made worse by the continued wet weather. We floundered along, up to the ankles in mud and mire, occasionally stepping into unseen holes so that our feet were always wet, and uncomfortable. Consequent on our steady increase of distance from rail-heads, rations soon began to be scarce and many a day we made a march varying from 18 to 25, or more, kilometres on nothing more to eat than one slice of bread, and a chunk of bully. Arrived at the end of the day's journey, we generally got a hot meal from the travelling cookers, and were left with our usual slice of bread or a biscuit for our breakfast before commencing our next day's march. In our nightly billets, of barns, and bare lofts, our wet socks were pulled off at night, and pulled on again in the same condition next morning, for it was rare that we could make fires to dry our clothes. There is no exaggeration when I say that I only used two pairs of socks in all the weeks of marching, and wore them wrong side and right side out in rotation. I was one of those fortunate enough to possess sound feet, yet even I suffered a lot, though not to compare with some poor fellows, who had blood oozing from their dilapidated boots at times, while on the march. We had to grin, and bear our hardships, and discomforts, while there was many an amusing episode on the journey, which caused us to laugh and forget temporarily, our many miseries. In every little village through which we passed, the inhabitants turned out en masse to give us welcome. Many places were decorated in carnival style, with triumphal arches erected over the roads bearing inscriptions such as 'Vive l'Angleterre', 'Vive l'Ecosse', while here and there, we came across effigies of the Kaiser, dressed in uniform and spiked helmet, hanging by the neck from the branch of a tree. The music of our two bands, especially that of the bag-pipes, appeared to delight the simple country folk, and as we passed through among them, we could hear them speak in awed voices with reference to our kilts which would no doubt excite their curiosity. The sound of the pipes was sufficient to bring all the people, old and young, to the roadside, to see us pass. Grey-haired men left their horses and ploughs in the field, and doffed their caps as we marched along, while fat old women with their children, came puffing and panting to see the 'bon Ecossais' and hear the 'belle musique'.

To return to the journey. When we arrived at Laneffe, a grand 'civic' reception awaited us. On nearing the village, we met a man with a bicycle, who, viewing us suddenly round a corner, promptly wheeled about, and dashed off as hard as he could pedal his machine. Evidently he was acting as a scout, for on approaching the outskirts of the village, we were met by a large crowd of people, at the head of which marched a band in full blast, the instruments composing which, seemed to have been of very ancient origin, if one might judge from their mouldy, verdigris, appearance. Our signal section, marching at the head of the battalion, would fain have burst out laughing, but respect for the good intentions of the welcoming villagers forbade it. At a sign from the C.O. Col Methuen, our pipers ceased playing, and without wasting any words, the strange-looking band of musicians, most of them old men, wheeled in front of us on the road, and at once struck up the French National Anthem. Marching ahead of us, they led the way into the village, where everybody seemed to be on holiday. Everywhere, there were decorations, whilst suspended in mid-air over the main thoroughfare hung a dummy figure representing the Kaiser, at which they pointed a scornful finger in evident glee. The afternoon was given up to great revelry, and in return for the hospitality shown us by the inhabitants, our brass and pipe bands played selections in the evening, while at intervals of an hour, the weird-looking village band headed a procession of joyful natives. We were now, of course, passing through the territory which had been under German rule for four years and, at Laneffe, were crossing eastern Belgium a few miles south of the big town of Charleroi. For a few days, we stayed among the villagers doing only a certain amount of light parades each day, till on the 24th we packed up again, and turning due east we marched to the little village called Stave. A night's rest here, and we went forward again next day to Weillen, a very pretty village hidden among the hills. Indeed, the scenery was becoming more beautiful, with every succeeding day's march towards the east, and had the weather been more favourable, we should have enjoyed the experience of passing through this new country much more. During our journey from Stave to Weillen, we passed a fine chateau standing in well-wooded grounds near the village of Servill, which, for some time previous to the Armistice, had been the headquarters of the German Crown

Prince. Just after passing Servill we traversed an s-shaped stretch of road, where the head and tail of the battalion were able to speak to each other in passing. At frequent intervals along the roadside, we came upon wrecked motor lorrys, and occasionally big guns abandoned by the Germans in their hurried flight to the 'fatherland'. We noticed too, that, with native thoroughness they had taken the precaution, in every instance, of making the abandoned material absolutely useless, except for scrap-iron, by setting fire to it or by exploding a bomb in a vital part of the machinery. We found also, in many cases, important bridges on the road had been mined so that our own army would be delayed as much as possible. Railways, too, especially at junctions had been bombed and mined, which caused the metals to assume fantastic shapes, one length of rail we saw being entwined round a chimney, in such a fashion as to resemble a gigantic snake. Such destruction, on the part of the beaten enemy, only served to show how intense was their spite and hatred against us, while it proved often enough a serious obstacle to our transport system. It became now a daily occurrence to meet men, who had been prisoners of war in the hands of the enemy, and were now cast aside by their captors, to live or die by the wayside, and poor, hungry, half starved men they were, of various nationalities, that included Britishers, French, Belgians and Italians. To these weary, wanderers, making their way westwards, we gave what we could from our own rations to help them on their way, but as we ourselves were never certain of receiving our food from one day to another, this became an added hardship, yet we were glad to do what we could to help the human flotsam of war that passed us by, day after day. We stayed at Weillen about a week, resting and cleaning up, for we were in a sad mess with travelling on the muddy roads. During this halt it was freely rumoured that the 1st Division was being withdrawn to take part in some great ceremonial procession in Paris, and thence to home, but the rumour never materialised. One afternoon, Sharp, Monteith, and I went into the pretty little town of Dinant, which stands on the banks of that famous river, the Meuse; a peaceful blue stream that winds its way with many a twist and turn among the hills. Standing high up on the further side of the river is the castle or fortress, built on a great natural foundation of solid rock, which appeared to rise sheer up from the edge of the Meuse. I remember, when we first glimpsed its bold outline, how we all remarked on its unusual similarity to the grand old pile of Edinburgh Castle. The old town of Dinant had suffered severely during the early days of the war, and to hinder the German advance at that time, the eastern half of the only bridge spanning the river had been blown up, but at the date of our visit a wooden structure had been erected to complete the bridge. All three of us spent a very pleasant afternoon of sightseeing, and enjoyed our tea of eggs, bread and coffee in a little cafe on the river-front. In the evening, as we walked back to Weillen we entered into conversation with a 'gendarme', who asked us if we cared to visit a famous 'Grotte' just off the road-side. As usual, ready for anything, we accepted his offer to act as guide, and were well repaid for our trouble to visit the caves, by the wonderful sights we saw there. The 'Grotte' or grotto was a series of caves containing marvellous formations of petrified rock, the whole ingeniously lit up by electric bulbs. These rocky petrifications had taken some strangely fantastic shapes in the various caverns, which were of lofty dimensions. One figure that specially took the eye was that of a great pulpit, with a wonderfully designed front, which glittered as if set with diamonds, and another in the pose of a woman lying asleep, which seemed very beautiful and natural. The echoes in the caves were awe-inspiring, and when we all laughed at the request of our guide, so that we might test the echoes, one would have thought that the devil himself had answered us, in the peals of wild laughter that reverberated and re-echoed through the vaults of the grotto. The *gendarme* explained to us that the 'Grotte' was, in ordinary times, a great attraction to tourists, but that during the war it had remained sealed up to prevent destruction by the invading Germans. We were very glad that our chance meeting with the gendarme had led to us seeing a most beautiful and wondrous place. Our return to billets was effected quietly, without anyone in authority knowing of our afternoon's 'French leave'. On another afternoon, we had plenty of excitement as spectators at a Rugby match, between a team of our own officers, and one from the officers of the Black Watch. Practically all the rank and file of both battalions were present, which was proof of the traditional rivalry of these two famous regiments. As might be expected no quarter was given or asked for. Every tackle and throw was wildly cheered, and when Lt A— of the Camerons collared Capt G— of the 'Watch' and stripped him of his sporting apparel from neck to knees in one wrench, the excitement was great. The gallant captain was hastily 'clothed' in a leather jerkin and continued, like a soldier should, but after a battle royal the Cameron officers proved victorious by 11 points to 3.

45
Marching eastwards

On December 1st, we left the village of Weillen, and continued our eastward march to Foy Notre Dame, passing through the town of Dinant on our way, the streets of which had been decorated with young ever-green trees in honour of the passing of the British forces. After leaving Dinant, we toiled upwards along rough roads, which were little removed from mountain passes for we were now among the mountainous country of the Ardennes, and heading for the boundary of Luxemburg. Such bad travelling had us well tired out by the time we had done the 16 kilometres that brought us to Foy. On top of the day's march I was Orderly Sgt, so that I got little rest, what with guard mounting, and running here and there with orders. There were no wires for me to look after now, all communications of any distance being done by motor-cycle despatch riders, while our cycle section looked after the shorter distances. After a night at Foy we marched a further 18 kilometres to Mont Gauthier, where the headquarter sections were billeted in the fine old monastry of that name. During our stay of a few days in the precincts of this great building, we were most hospitably treated by the monks who lived there. These quiet, serious looking men took a pleasure in showing us over the monastery, and appeared to be proud to have us as their guests. At their invitation, our two bands provided a musical afternoon in one of the larger rooms, at which all the regimental officers were present, and many of us headquarter fellows contrived to be there also, unobserved by the officers. The monks seemed to enjoy the entertainment; so did we, also the wine they handed round at frequent intervals. Our officer's mess was in the adjacent nunnery, and in the course of my duties as O. S. I had the opportunity of seeing inside the beautiful dining-room, with its complement of silver, which had been placed at the disposal of the officers during the stay of the regiment. While here, the nuns took a great fancy to the tartan ribbons that adorned the bag-pipes, and were delighted when Pipe-Major Scotland presented them with some Cameron tartan. It was during our halt, at the monastry of Mont Gauther, that the regimental colours were brought out to us from Edinburgh Castle. To us soldiers of the new army they were a sight to see. The list of battle honours inscribed on the regimental colour are second to none, and with the King's Colour, are symbolical of the great fighting records of the 79th Regiment of Foot. At all times, both at home and abroad, were the colours jealously guarded, and on their arrival at the monastry, the colours were unfurled and hung in a room where we could all inspect them, under the vigilant eye of a sentry. Later, Col Methuen, who was very ill, but insisted on accompanying the regiment conveyed in a motor ambulance, gave a lecture to the battalion on the history of the colours.

On December 7th, we left our good friends at Mont Gauther, and took the road to Haversin only 7 kilometres distant, the reason for such a short journey being the difficulty encountered in securing sufficient billeting accommodation for the whole battalion, but it must not be thought that now the war was over, we had nice apartments and good clean beds to sleep in. On the contrary, we were at times lucky to have a roof over our heads, while now the weather was of more than usual severity, accentuated in no little manner, by reason of the high altitudes we had now reached. Often, marching in the rain, or through blinding snowstorms, we were wet to the skin when halted for the night. On occasions, we did manage to build a fire, more often we rose in the morning cold and wet, as we had lain down the night before. We carried no clothes except what we wore, save perhaps a shirt. All surplus articles we threw away, bit by bit, to lighten our load on the journey. Besides clothing, which we could ill afford to lose, these often included treasured souvenirs, which had been carried about by men for months, and even years. But now, it was a test of endurance to continue the terrible march at all. One day, when crossing over high hills by a rough roadway, we asked to keep going on when halting time came, rather than sit starving by the wayside, in the blizzard which was raging. Continuing our march on Sunday December 8th, we tramped a distance of 15 kilometres, from Haversin to Noiseux in wet, disagreeable weather and over extremely bad roads. Another day's march found us crossing the Luxemburg frontier, and after a journey of 14 kilometres, we came to the village of Bomal, where a halt was again called for three days, during which, the regimental shoe-makers had a busy time repairing our footwear which, in many instances, was greatly in need of their attentions. Wild weather continued, and, combined with the rough wretched roads, caused a certain amount of distress in the ranks, so that a few days of rest now and then was necessary and welcome. Since leaving Mont Gauther we had taken a north-easterly route, and the mountainous country, through which we were passing, would have impressed us greatly with its magnificent scenery had the climatic conditions been more favourable. As it was, many of the splendid panoramic views, of mountain and valley, forest and stream, were worthy rivals of the finest scenes in the Scottish Highlands, though now in the icy grip of winter they presented rather a cold, bleak, menacing aspect. Towns were scarce, and villages lay in valleys lying far apart. It was remarkable too how pro-German the people appeared to be, the nearer we approached the German frontier. In many of the villages through which we passed, the inhabitants hurried into their houses, and closed the doors, directly they saw us marching towards them, and from their curtained windows watched, with sullen faces, our passage down the deserted village street. Their manners were in great contrast to those of the people in the liberated French and Belgian villages, who had welcomed us so warmly. It may have been that the natives of the borderland were afraid we should harm them, but their sour, sullen dispositions did not point towards fear of us. They never seemed anxious to oblige us in billeting, or assisting in any ways we might have hoped for, from which we concluded there was too much German blood amongst them, to be friendly with British soldiers.

Leaving Bomal on the 13th, we took the road again, and marched in a downpour of rain to Bihain a distance of 14 kilometres. We stayed there overnight only, and next morning, wet and uncomfortable as we were, we plodded on along slushy roads in continued heavy rain to the village of Grandmesnil, distant 17 kilometres. We were thankful when that day's march was over, and we were safely into a dry shelter.

46
Crossing the German frontier

Only one nights rest, and a short sleep at Grandmesnil, then off we went again another 14 kilometres to Rogery, the little group of scattered dwellings, which was to mark our last billet before stepping on to German soil. Now that we had got so near to Germany, there was naturally a good deal of excitement amongst us. At last we were about to enter the territory of our late enemy, and in conjuring up thoughts of what that great country would be like, our hardships and trials endured on the journey were momentarily forgotten. Germany, which to us seemed a sort of promised land lay ahead of us and our enthusiasm was centred on the future, for soon we hoped to reach our journey's end. Monday 16th December, was a memorable day for the 1st Cameron Highlrs for on that morning, one hours march from Rogery, we came in sight of the German frontier. The distinguishing mark was a tall, thick post, erected on the grassy border of the road side, which was painted with the German national colours, red, white and black in such a fashion, as to resemble a huge barber's pole stuck in the ground. We halted for our usual ten minute's rest on the Luxemburg side of the boundary, and here we were told that we should cross the frontier in a manner befitting the regiment – with bayonets fixed and colours flying.

The ceremony was one that will live long in the memories of the men taking part in it. At the end of our ten minutes rest, we formed up in line on the road, then the Colonel mounted on his charger gave the order in his high ringing voice – 'Fix!... Bayonets!...' As the right hand man of the Hq Coy, the honour fell to me to give 'the time', for this memorable fixing of bayonets. Six smart steps forward, which placed me in full view of the battalion in line, then with rifle gripped between the knees I waited while every man, feeling for the hilt of his bayonet, kept his eye on me for the next move. There followed a noticeable loosening of the bayonets, then there sounded a swish of steel as a thousand blades flashed from their scabbards, followed immediately by a rattle, as they were snapped and locked on the muzzles of the rifles. One more simultaneous movement, and the regiment was braced up to 'attention', and in a moment I had regained my position on the right of the line. It had been a grand 'fix' and one to be proud of, but I confess my knees quivered when it was over. Swiftly now came the order 'Battalion!... Slope!... Arms!' In another instant the colours were unfurled and fluttered majestically in the breeze, and this was the signal for the next order, 'Present!... Arms!' and in that position we stood in salute to the colours while the band played our National Anthem. Then the voice of the C.O. was heard again, 'Slope!... Arms! Form!... Fours! Right! By the right! Quick!... March!' There was a crash and rattle of drums, the pipers played our famous march, the '79ths Farewell', and precisely at 10.20am, with heads held high, and colours flying, we crossed the line into Germany. Some little distance across the frontier a tall flag-staff had been erected from the top of which the 'Union Jack' floated proudly. Grouped near it were the Brigadiers and Staff Officers of the 1st Division, while in front of them, taking the salute as the battalion marched by, stood the tall, white-haired, soldierly figure of the Divisional Commander, General Strickland. I have recollections of shortly afterwards leaving the main road, and floundering through the mud of a very dirty lane to our billets in the small hamlet of Aldringen. Our day's march had only measured 10 kilometres, but it was certainly one of the most prominent days in our army careers. One night was all we stayed in Aldringen, and next morning we resumed our march in the midst of heavy rain and facing a bitterly, cold wind which blew from the east and chilled us through and through. We put in a good day's tramp of 29 kilometres which tired us greatly before reaching the town of Setz. On the way we had passed through many villages, where the natives watched us curiously from the shelter of their doorways as we passed. Fat, old, fraus, and children whose bullet-heads and flaxen-hued hair were unmistakably German, stared as if they recognised in us, the 'Devil's Ladies', as the Kaiser himself had named us, and wondering if we should suddenly turn and commit atrocities among them.

47
The end of the trail

The little town of Setz was left behind on December 18th, and we continued our march through sleet and snow a further 20 kilometres to another small town named Halleschlag. It will be noticed that our daily marches were now being extended in length, and this, together with the abnormal severity of the winter, and only having a night's rest between most of the hard days of tramping, made us weary and in some cases exhausted. There was a good deal of 'grousing' against everything in general that pertained to the march, and against the weather in particular. Even the natives of the district remarked on its unusual hardness and said it was years since they had even had a fall of snow approaching the dimensions of that which we had recently experienced. From Halleschlag, we went forward the following day to the village of Schmidtheim, a distance of 15 kilometres, and here, we halted for two days in order that the worst of boots could be repaired. I, for one was glad of this halt as my boots were almost worn off my feet, and bad boots on bad roads doubled the hardships of the march. At Schmidtheim, the battalion was billeted in the farm buildings of the village, while the different sections comprising the Hqr Coy found quarters in a fine old country mansion. We signallers occupied the billiard room which I recollect, chiefly because it contained a very large stove which served to warm the room excellently, and also because of its lavish, and brilliant electric lighting arrangements. In the centre of the room under a great cluster of electric bulbs stood a large billiard table, while the walls were graced with valuable old tapestries. Portraits of lords and ladies, probably ancestors of the resident family, looked down on us from their huge gilt frames, and in the warmth and comfort of that great room, we spent two restful nights rolled in our blankets on the floor with our packs doing duty as pillows. In other rooms, we discovered more valuable pictures and furniture, and in one large room which was fitted up after the style of a museum, we saw a large collection of trophies of hunting, and shooting expeditions. Large boars' heads, and the horns and antlers of various wild beasts garnished the walls of this apartment, with stuffed birds and many small animals being arranged artistically in glass cases round the room.

On occasions, we saw the German Count who owned and occupied this grand house. During the first night of our stay he, poor man, had the misfortune to be arrested by the sentry on duty at the entrance to the grounds for being out of doors after 9pm, in contravention of martial law, and duly passed the night in the regimental guard-room, while we were sleeping serenely in his stately mansion. He was, of course, not the only person caught on the prowl and kept a prisoner all night. Some of these may have been out with a legitimate purpose, some were certainly out with no good intentions, and the safest plan was to put them all under arrest when found prowling about after the specified hour, of nine o'clock.

Our brief rest at Schmidtheim was marked by heavy falls of snow, so that we were very thankful to have a comfortable shelter for the time being. Early on the morning of the 21st December however we rolled our blankets, packed up our kits and set off on another stage of the journey to the banks of the Rhine. A long march of 28 kilometres brought us at an early hour in the afternoon to the town of Munstereifel. A halt for one night only, gave us small chance of exploring this town, and as a matter-of-fact, we were much too tired to want to go far. We had not so far been able to pick up more than a word or two of the German dialect, and we often found ourselves in comical situations, when trying to make out what the natives said to us. The language of signs however in many cases came to our rescue, one instance being when Duff Grant, a signaller, having exhausted his knowledge of both English and French in a vain endeavour to beg some hot water from a 'frau', with which to bathe his feet had the happy inspiration of showing the bewildered woman his sore feet and handing her a bucket, and in a short time the desired hot water was forthcoming accompanied by a lot of German language that was probably a well-meant expression of sympathy. Gradually as we progressed eastwards the German people were becoming less hostile towards us. No doubt in their war propaganda, the German War Lords had instilled into the minds of many of these simple peasant populace, a very black picture of the conduct and habits of the British soldier, but as they became better acquainted with us, they found out we were not by any means as black as we had been painted. From Munstereifel, we pushed on again after a night's rest to Kuckenheim, a distance of 14 kilometres. Latterly we had left the hilly district of the borderland and were now entering the more level country which ultimately merges into the valley of the great river of Germany, the Rhine. The 23rd of December brought us to the end of our long weary march, for on that date the final 20 kilometres between Kuckenheim and the pleasant little village of Waldorf was traversed, and we found ourselves within sight of, and four miles distant, from the banks of the Rhine. It was a great relief to know that at long last we had reached our goal. In all, we had marched the equivalent of 250 English miles, under the worst possible conditions, as regards weather and roads, while with one or two exceptions, our periods of rest had been of the most brief description, so it was small wonder that we experienced a sense of thankfulness, in coming to rest at the end of a great and wonderful journey.

For one night, part of the signal section was billeted in the house of the village post-master of Waldorf and occupied one of the rooms upstairs. Barely had we established ourselves there, when orders came for a guard to be mounted on the main road between Cologne and Bonn, and as our billet stood at a convenient cross-roads, it fell to me to take charge of a guard of signallers. Our duties were to see that no civilians prowled about the village after 9pm, also to stop all vehicles, examine their contents and see that the passports, of those in charge, duly authorised them to travel. 'Herr' Kurtz, the postmaster very obligingly allowed us to have the use of his kitchen for a guardroom and when, in spite of our display of rifles and fixed bayonets, together with other warlike weapons, they recognised that we were, after all, only a harmless lot of fellows, the entire family became very friendly towards us. 'Frau' Kurtz was a motherly old soul who furnished us with a bounteous supply of hot coffee and black bread for our refreshment during the night watches, which was indeed very acceptable, for own rations would not allow of meals by night as well as by day. Nothing of an exciting nature happened during our period of guard, and the only people challenged by the sentry pacing the road outside, were a few market-gardeners, who, with their high, four-wheeled carts filled with freshly-gathered vegetables were making an early-morning start for the markets in Cologne, and as they had all the necessary papers, permitting them to travel, we had no trouble with any of them, but after a hard day's march and no sleep I was glad when our time expired next morning.

48

A few weeks in Germany

During the following day, we moved our billets from Waldorf to the adjoining village called Dersdorf, where we were billeted among the inhabitants in twos and threes instead of the usual sections being placed in empty houses and outbuildings. Jimmy Sharp and I went, inseparable companions to the end, to stay with an old hard working farmer named Braunn. His wife, a stout, fussy, kind old 'frau' seemed to take to us both, from the moment we entered the house, and I can picture the old woman showing us the little bedroom she placed at our disposal, and bringing us clean white sheets to use. On the ground-floor the little back-kitchen, normally her own snug domain, was handed over to us, and here we took our meals, while every day she kept a fire burning for our benefit. In the evenings, after his day's work was done, the old German obviously a little shy at first, liked nothing better than to come in and sit by the fireside, in order that he might talk with us. Sharp was himself a farmer's son, so that farming made a favourite subject for conversation, though almost every word on both sides required its explanation in signs, and consequently talking was a slow business. However, with the assistance of the old farmer's niece, a school-girl, we made astonishing progress. The war was a topic that was very rarely mentioned between us, but Herr Braunn was delighted to hear anything about 'Schotland', as he called it. Besides helping greatly to while away the long winter evenings, these conversations assisted us in picking up a fair amount of German language. The village of Dersdorf lay in the midst of a rich agricultural district which was part of the great valley of the Rhine, while the river of that name could be seen in the distance winding northwards like a thread of silver between the two towns of Bonn and Cologne. A feature of the district was the light railway, which ran along the hedge on the roadside. The little trains which came chugging along at frequent intervals formed a convenient means of transport for the population of the country villages. In every house both large and small, appeared an installation of electric light, even the cow-sheds, and stables at the farm where we were billeted, were electrically illuminated. The people, however, without a doubt, were of a thrifty, careful, nature and lived in a most frugal manner. We saw no delicacies on their table at meal times, but good soups and stews with black bread and coffee of a similar hue were greatly in evidence. One thing they had in plenty, which surprised us, was loaf sugar, an item which at that time could hardly be purchased at home in England. Quite as surprising, to their eyes, were the loaves of good white bread which daily were issued to us as part of rations. Having now a regularly forthcoming issue of food, Sharp and I often gave Frau Braunn a piece of white bread, which pleased her immensely. Now that the battalion was fairly settled we prepared to have a good time while we stayed in Germany.

On Christmas night, a grand dance was arranged to take place in the village concert room, and the young ladies of the village and neighbourhood were invited, but most of them declined to dance on that night because they spent most part of Christmas Day at church. I remember the Braunn family attended service no fewer than seven times that day. To us the day was spent as a holiday except for Church Parade, but we had no grand Xmas dinner. The dance at night was the scene of great hilarity and the scarcity of ladies did not upset the arrangements, nor prevent us enjoying ourselves thoroughly. The days that followed were spent in quiet training, more for the sake of exercise than for any other purpose I think. Since arriving at Dersdorf, I had been continually acting as Hq Orderly Sergeant which, now that the regiment occupied settled billets, was a nice easy job and kept me away from the ordinary work of the battalion. In addition to attending to orders, twice daily I went round the various billets collecting the mens' letters, and consequently saw into a good many German homes, and met a large number of the inhabitants. In one of the houses a woman showed me the 'Iron Cross' won by her son, who had afterwards been killed in action. Naturally, his mother was very proud of her son's decoration, and would not allow it to leave her hands. Generally speaking, the older folk were friendly, but the young men, of whom a good number were beginning to return home from their military duties, we did not trust too far. In conversation with these returned soldiers, we found, in some cases, they had been in action against us at certain times and places, but the remarkable thing about many of them was, that they would not admit having been fighting soldiers, but wanted us to believe they had all been R.A.M.C., or Transport men. Perhaps they were afraid we should 'go for them' if they owned up to being 'fighters'.

On New Year's Day 1919, Sharp, Monteith, and myself took a walk to the banks of the Rhine. Straight across country we went, only pausing here and there to admire the scenery of the beautiful Rhine Valley. Across the level country we could obtain splendid views of the grass lands, dotted here and there with pleasant looking red-roofed farm houses, and groups of poplars that betrayed the presence of small hamlets. Sharp said 'he wouldn't mind five hundred acres of the valley for a farm', and from a farming point of view I doubt if the land of the Rhine district could be beaten. After a good walk we reached the banks of the river, of which we had heard and talked so much during the years of war. It was now in heavy flood, its discoloured waters rushing along in a mighty volume to the sea. For some minutes we stood in silence, gazing at the foaming torrent, which represented the border line, beyond which the British and Allied Armies must not pass. 'Well' said Sharp, as he solemnly took his watch from his pocket, and proceeded to wind it up, 'Its taken us a long, long time, but at least, like the song, we can always say, "We've wound up the watch on the Rhine"'. Returning from the river at a brisk pace, we arrived at our billets in Dersdorf in time to take part in the New Year celebrations, which took the form of a grand dinner. My company (D) had been successful in securing a school-room for this great occasion, and provisions and wine being provided on a liberal scale, we did justice to the feast and enjoyed ourselves thoroughly. The dinner was a prolonged affair and the arrival of the commanding officer, Colonel Methuen in the midst of the rejoicings, was the signal for a spontaneous outburst of enthusiastic welcome for the chief of the regiment. In a short speech, replying to his vociferous reception, the C.O. said, 'It has been a proud honour to have led such a great fighting regiment as the 1st Cameron Highlanders, and all through the greatest war the world has ever known you have worthily upheld in many fierce actions the regimental motto, – "A Cameron never can yield"'. On his proposal of the toast of 'The King' every man stood to attention, with his glass in hand, but before we could drink, 'Old Joe' the grey-haired, be-ribboned, old warrior at the head of the table cried out, in that ringing stentorian voice we all knew so well, 'Up! Up! Every man of you and drink it with Highland honours' and suiting the action to the word every one sprang up, and with one foot on the chair and one on top of the table, we drank the toast in typical Highland fashion. More speeches from 'Old Joe' and other senior non-commissioned-officers, and songs and choruses from individuals, and the company respectively helped to pass a happy afternoon.

This, my fourth New Year's Day abroad has provided probably the most pleasant memories of all. The others, 1916 at Lillers, 1917 on the Somme battlefield, and 1918, in the line at Houthulst Forest had all been spent, more or less, under conditions of great hardships and dangers, but now in 1919 our fighting days were finished and once again we were living under peaceable and fairly comfortable conditions of soldiering, so we made merry as part of a victorious army.

We jogged along very quietly during the days following the great dinner of New Year's Day, and in my capacity of Orderly Sergeant I had perhaps an easier time than most. After the battalion had gone off for a route-march in the mornings, I was more or less free till guard mounting in the evening, and this, under 'Old Joe's' command, was in the nature of a ceremony. Everything in dress, in arms, and the prescribed method of changing guard had to be exact, and woe betide the unlucky sentry, or sergeant of the guard, who did not perform his duties smartly. When the pipe band assembled in the evening to play 'Retreat' there was always a crowd of wondering civilians to listen to the skirling pipes, and watch the masterly display of the drummers. Often in the hours of leisure, I went down to visit the old postmaster in Waldorf and was always made welcome in his house. Frau Kurtz, his wife, always insisted on giving me something to eat, no matter what time of day I appeared and many a cup of coffee and new-laid egg, I enjoyed as the result of her hospitality. The Kurtz family consisted of two girls the Frauleins Katrina and Kristina, and two very nice girls they were. Katrina the elder stayed at home with her mother and was, at the same time, the devoted nurse of her old grandmother who was a gentle-minded invalid lady, confined to bed. Kristina a clever girl of 16 years was employed in the village post-office, and from the night when we occupied their kitchen as a guard-room, both girls had been very kind, and friendly. The lively Kristina was anxious to learn 'English', and ever-ready to have a talk with me. There was the natural difficulty at first of making oneself understood, but with the aid of a dictionary, of German–English composition we got on wonderfully, while the old people looked on and smiled as we puzzled our way through to speaking terms. Sometimes Sharp would go with me in the evenings and we spent many happy hours in the company of our German friends, in their little home at Waldorf.

49
Coming home

We had now reached the period when a number of men were departing for home almost daily, some going on leave, while others, who were able to prove satisfactorily that they had work to go to, left the battalion for good. The thought of so many old companions gradually dwindling away from the regiment made the remainder of us feel restless also. So far I had not made any application to go home to my work, knowing I was due any day for leave, and decided to wait till that time. As things were I was having quite a nice time of it just then, and apart from the fact I should certainly have been pleased to see everybody at home, there was no real need for me to hurry back to England, so I just waited patiently for my leave, meanwhile attending to the duties of O. Sergeant for Headquarters.

At last, however, my name appeared in orders at the end of January to proceed home on leave, and it was then I realised that the time had come for the final parting with all the old pals, with the good old '79th', and that my career of soldiering was soon to come to an end. On the afternoon previous to the day I had to leave for home, the RS Major 'Old Joe', called me aside and said 'I go on leave tomorrow also, corporal, will you go along with me, and help me with my kit?' I readily agreed and then he suggested, that instead of going direct to Cologne, as, according to the route laid down, we ought to have done, we should take the wayside

railway to Bonn, and travel from there to Cologne by the fine electric railway, which ran in close proximity to the banks of the
Rhine, which method would afford us an excellent view of the
river between the two towns. This was a good idea, and possibly by
reason of his rank, I appreciated his practical kindness. In the
evening, I paid a farewell visit to the Kurtz family in Waldorf, and
they were all sorry, the girls especially, that I was going home. Herr
Braunn, and his good wife too, were surprised when I said I was
coming back no more. In the morning, my kit was packed up for
the journey, and I went round the signal section to say the final
'Goodbyes'. Jimmy Sharp and Monteith as my special friends,
found it hard to keep up under the emotions of wishing me luck,
and a long gripping hand-shake, and I too felt the parting as in that
brief moment I recalled all we had gone through shoulder to
shoulder. On my way to the little station where I was to meet 'Old
Joe', I met the padre, who seeing I was bound for home, wished me
luck, and shook hands. Then when I believed I was clear of the
battalion at last who should I meet but the Signal Officer. 'Good
morning Jackson' he said, 'are you really going?' 'Yes Sir' I
answered. 'Coming back?' he asked after a slight pause. 'No Sir', said
I as bravely as I could. 'You know it means sergeant's stripes for
you, if you do', he said (I had been made corporal some time
before), but I shook my head. The call for home was just a little too
strong for me then and my mind was made up to finish once I got
back to England. He shook hands and wished me luck in the future
and I'm sure there was mutual regret in our parting, for besides
being officer and man we had been the best of friends. Joining the
train at Dersdorf, it did not take long to reach the fine looking
town of Bonn, and in the company of 'Old Joe' I had a short walk
along the main thoroughfares, and admired the large well built
public buildings and smart shopping centres of the town; but being
greatly hampered with our heavy kits and the three days rations we
each carried in addition, we soon got tired of sight seeing, and so
we made our way to the station. Taking the electric train from
there we were carried swiftly along to Cologne. The roundabout

way as suggested by the Sgt-Major was certainly worth while, and I fully enjoyed the trip alongside the Rhine, whose winding river remained in view all the time. Arrived at Cologne, our attention was immediately drawn to the famous cathedral easily recognised by its fine architecture and the height of its spire. The splendidly constructed Rhine bridges, for which Cologne is justly famous, were also prominent features, at each of which could be noticed strong guards of British soldiers. We did not, however, spend much time in sight-seeing, but made our way to the great main railway station, at the entrance to which we saw a large hole where the street had been damaged by a bomb from a British aeroplane. In the station we sat down to rest and wait for the leave train due to leave about midnight. While having a meal from sandwiches, which 'Old Joe' brought out of his haversack, we found much to interest us in the hurry and bustle always associated with a great railway centre. There were scores of British and Colonial soldiers, all like ourselves, bound for home, all in jovial mood at the prospect, for the majority at least, of going home for good.

The train, when it did eventually come alongside the platform, was a poor affair, having uncomfortably-hard, wooden seats and without any heating apparatus attached to the carriages. A cold miserable journey it proved to be as we crawled slowly westwards during the dark hours of night in the direction of France. The first town of importance we stopped at was Aix-la-Chapelle near the German–Belgian frontier, and from there we passed on till we reached the town of Leige, that large manufacturing point of Eastern Belgium. Turning south-west and following the line of the River Meuse, which we crossed and recrossed several times, as we passed through a mountainous district of great scenic beauty, we came to the old fortress town of Namur one the first places to suffer destruction from German guns during the war. Viewed from the train, the fortress of earlier days was simply a grey pile of ruins, and from this town, as we journeyed westwards we were crossing the battle area, where every town and village we saw was more or less a ruin, and every ridge and valley was seared with a maze of trenches, that were now deserted. Iron stakes, with battered and broken lines of defensive wire twisted about them, showed where the barriers against sudden attack on front line trenches had been erected by both armies, and these barbed-wire entanglements showed how effective artillery fire had been. On all sides the ground was pock-marked with shell holes and craters, some large, some small, while amid the general desolation could be seen those little wooden crosses standing like miniature sentries guarding the mounds of earth, which denoted the resting places of good men killed in action. The whole district gave the impression of a wilderness and a cemetery merged into the same area. On the railway near Charleroi, which town could be seen on our right we noticed the remains of a long train which had either suffered from a bombing expedition, or been caught by gun fire. All that was left of it resembled a long heap of scrap iron. Outside of Valenciennes, we were held up long enough to be able to leave the train, and stretch our legs in a brisk walk. In a convenient shell-hole I found some passably clean water, and had a wash and shave, and also took the opportunity of helping the Sgt Major to make himself spic and span. Throughout the journey 'Old Joe' had proved a genial companion, and was ever ready to do his share in helping to pass the time, by singing a song or spinning a yarn. From the stern old fire-eater of a Sgt Major, whose word was law in the battalion he ruled with rigid discipline, he had, since leaving the regiment, become a mild-mannered old man – just a soldier going home on leave, and as happy as a youngster on a Sunday School trip. On the second night of our journey we reached Douai and here we were allowed to leave the train, for the purpose of visiting the large dry canteen erected near the station. In it, we were able to purchase a decent meal which we were all badly needing. The counters, and the men serving behind them, were besieged by scores of hungry men, and it took a long time to supply our various requirements. From Douai, the remainder of the journey was across a district we knew almost yard by yard, and each succeeding point brought with it a full quota of memories, some of sadness, others that were pleasant to remember. In that secluded tract, we had played at football, and on those slopes we had cut and thrust with bayonets for dear life. What contrasting recollections each sector of the north of France had provided. For more than four years I had been going up and down and in and out of those trenches, and now this was the final crossing. Our journey by train came to its conclusion, on the third day, at Calais, and here my last link with the 1st Camerons was broken, as 'Old Joe' fell in with friends, and after thanking me for accompanying him 'down the line', said he should manage alright among his friends as far as London. In a camp, specially provided for men going on leave, we attended to our toilets and enjoyed a good dinner in hearty fashion.

Later in the afternoon, we boarded the ship that was to carry us back to England and home. The short crossing to Dover was by far the worst I had ever experienced, with the white-topped waters of the Channel running mountains high, so that it seemed any minute we should founder in the trough of angry sea.

Long before we sighted the chalk-white cliffs that marked the longed-for shores of 'Old England', we were all soaking wet to the skin and chilled to the bones with the waves and flying spray that lashed the little steamer from stem to stern as she rode the mighty billows. I stood in the stern trying my best to brave the elements, but the heaving and tossing in the end made me violently sick so that I was glad indeed to step off the boat on to solid ground again. Trains, ready at the harbour station, quickly whirled us up to London, and there was nothing to do but wait for the night express to Carlisle.

After five days of almost continual travel I was home again. I had not sent any word that I was returning; there hadn't been time for that, and in any case it would have taken a letter almost as long to come as myself.

I walked the few miles from the city to my own home and still in the early morning hours before the quiet old village was stirring to its daily work. I'll always remember knocking at the door, and in reply to the question from the window above – 'Who's that?', I startled my mother by saying, 'It's Jack, I've come home'.

The welcome that followed is not for description here neither could it be understood except by those, who, like myself, went away when the country called us, and were spared through all the struggles of war to return safely home again.

I was indeed fortunate in returning as fit and in the same good health as when I went away. At long last the Great War was over; through it I had travelled various parts of Europe that I had never hoped to see under ordinary circumstances, foreign places and strange people that most fellows like myself only read about in books and newspapers. What had I learned from my war experiences? Many, many, facts, first of which I should say in the words of an old song 'There's no place like Home', nor any country like our native Britain.

I should say also that war brings out the worst and also the best in men.

Not all men can stand the horror and the hardness of war, some are shown up to be selfish, craven, cowards, many more are proved to be made of the best stuff, men who would sacrifice even life itself to save a friend without the slightest hesitation. Heroes every one of them. There were the friends you could depend on, men you were proud to have known, like my own good pals Jimmy Monteith and Jimmy Sharp. I mention their names here deliberately, as a little tribute to two grand comrades-in-arms. They will read this book and I feel sure they will understand.

Men and incidents have left their mark on my memory. Here are some taken at random. My first Commanding Officer Lt Col Douglas-Hamilton VC who died at the head of his men at Loos, with his Adjutant Capt Milne. The embarkation and landing of the Camerons at Le Havre, and our first spell in the trenches. The roll-call of the Camerons in the garden by R.S.M. Peter Scotland after Loos. The sail from Rouen up the River Seine in a hospital ship. The Hospital at Monifieth and the fine time at Stirling. The day I proudly joined the 1st Cameron Highlanders. R.S. Major Sydney

Axton with all his decorations, the 'Perfect Model of a Perfect Soldier'. The pipes and drums of the battalion playing 'Retreat' in quiet French villages. The regimental colours which flew unfurled as we entered Germany. The 'Fix-Bayonets' command as we crossed the Frontier. The calm blue eyes of General Strickland as he shook my hand on the field at Woeston, the mud and the blood of the trenches and the morning of the 11th November 1918 when war ended. These men and things I shall not forget.

50

Conclusion

Before my period of leave expired I interviewed with officials of the Railway Company in Glasgow regarding the prospect of being recalled from military duties and was gladly surprised to find that my discharge from the army had been applied for, and the necessary documents must have crossed me on my way home from Germany.

It was during this visit I encountered Malcolm McLeod one of the three friends who joined up with me in 1914. He looked well, after 2 years as a prisoner of war in Germany. I learned from him that Joe Symes had been discharged through wounds in action, so that of the four of us only one, poor Andrew Johnstone, had made the supreme sacrifice.

In due course, I had orders to proceed to Ripon Camp in Yorkshire for demobilisation and there handed in my rifle and equipment but retained my kilt as a memento of army days.

Having received my discharge papers I was once again a civilian and, after a short holiday, resumed my former employment on the railway.

✳ ✳ ✳ ✳ ✳

Some few weeks after I had finally left the army, I was one day summoned to Carlisle Castle and there, in the presence of a few friends, and with a small Guard of Honour supplied by the Border Regt, the decoration of the Military Medal was presented to me, for duty done during those terrible hours on Passchendale Ridge.

I suppose that day should stand out above all others in my army career, but during the ceremony I could only wistfully think of that other day in the field at Woeston, of the 'tartan square' of Black Watch and Camerons standing at the 'Present Arms', and the words of the General as we shook hands. That was my day.

Here my reminiscences must end. If the reading of them can only give as much pleasure to the reader as the writing of them has afforded me, I shall be well satisfied.

It is now the year 1926 and almost twelve years since I set off on my life's 'Great Adventure', and if there is one thing above others that I am proud of, then surely it was the happy choice that placed me in the ranks of 'The Queen's Own Cameron Highlanders', whose record in battle is second to none, and as a regiment are well worthy of their famous motto:

Whatever Men Dare, They Can Do!

INDEX